NOBLE DAUGHTERS

**Recent Titles in
Contributions to the Study of Religion**

NOBLE DAUGHTERS

Unheralded Women in Western Christianity, 13th to 18th Centuries

Marie A. Conn

Contributions to the Study of Religion, Number 60

GREENWOOD PRESS
Westport, Connecticut • London

Library of Congress Cataloging-in-Publication Data

Conn, Marie A., 1944–
   Noble daughters : unheralded women in western Christianity, 13th
to 18th centuries / Marie A. Conn.
      p.   cm.—(Contributions to the study of religion, ISSN
0196-7053 ; no. 60)
   Includes bibliographical references and index.
   ISBN 0-313-30669-9 (alk. paper)
   1. Women—Religious life—History.   2. Women in Christianity—
History.   3. Beguines—Belgium—History.   4. Witches—Europe—
History.   5. Anabaptist women—Europe—History.   6. Nuns—France—
Paris—History.   7. Women—History—Middle Ages, 500–1500.
8. Women—History—Renaissance, 1450–1600.   9. Women—History—17th
century.   10. Women—History—18th century.   I. Title.   II. Series.
BV639.W7C58   2000
270'.082—dc21   99–22142

British Library Cataloguing in Publication Data is available.

Library of Congress Catalog Card Number: 99–22142
ISBN: 0-313-30669-9
ISSN: 0196-7053

First published in 2000

Greenwood Press, 88 Post Road West, Westport, CT 06881
An imprint of Greenwood Publishing Group, Inc.
www.greenwood.com

Printed in the United States of America

The paper used in this book complies with the
Permanent Paper Standard issued by the National
Information Standards Organization (Z39.48–1984).

10 9 8 7 6 5 4 3 2 1

Copyright Acknowledgments

The author and publisher gratefully acknowledge permission for use of the following material:

Four quotes, set apart, from *Witchcraze: A New History of the European Witch
Hunts* by Anne Llewellyn Barstow. Copyright © 1994 by Anne Llewellyn Barstow.
Reprinted by permission of HarperCollins Publishers, Inc.

for my mother,
Alice St. Onge Conn,
unheralded but never unloved

Contents

Preface

Several years ago, when I first began to think seriously about the project that eventually became this book, I shared my idea with F. Ellen Weaver, a former colleague at Notre Dame and the leading American authority on the nuns of the monastery of Port-Royal in Paris. Ellen wished me well, but observed that the women of Port-Royal "didn't fit" with the other groups I intended to include. Although I took her comment seriously, I decided to plunge in and let the research make the decision. My conclusion was that these four groups of women did indeed "fit" together, not because their experiences were exactly similar, but because they envisioned a particular way of living a Christian life and remained true to that vision in the face of daunting obstacles and opposition.

Thanks are due in a special way to Cathy Lavin, a friend for many years, who spent precious hours reading, critiquing, and supporting; to Regis Duffy, OFM, my mentor at Notre Dame, who never stopped believing in me; to Carol Consorto, the intrepid handler of interlibrary loan requests at Chestnut Hill College, without whom I would have faced formidable obstacles myself; to Pamela St. Clair and Elizabeth Meagher, editors at Greenwood Press, both of whom have been understanding of unforeseen delays; and, most of all, to the women who inspired me with their lives and stories, the women you will meet in these pages.

Introduction

Go up onto a high mountain,
    Zion, herald of glad tidings;
Cry out at the top of your voice,
    Jerusalem, herald of good news! (Isaiah 40:9)

In ancient times, a herald was the officer who made state or royal proclamations, bearing ceremonial messages between princes and powers. Biblically, the herald was the one who brought good news as a ruler's representative or who announced the king's presence or will.[1]

The birth of an important person, a hero, a liberator, a savior would obviously be "good news," so in the Bible such births were announced by heralds. Perhaps it should not come as a surprise to learn that no woman's birth was thus proclaimed.

In discussing Exodus 2:1–2, Phyllis Trible underscores the text's implication that Moses is the firstborn child in his family: "A man from the house of Levi went and took a daughter of Levi. The woman conceived and bore a son." Yet, two verses later, we learn the infant has a sister old enough to be entrusted with watching his cradle as it nests among the reeds along the banks of the river. That sister, who remains nameless throughout this incident, is Miriam. Unheralded, unnamed, voiceless, Miriam "enters Scripture obliquely. No lineage, birth announcement, or naming ritual proclaims her advent. Only silence gives her birth."[2] Yet Miriam will play a vital role in the liberation of the Hebrews from Egypt, will be known as a prophet and a leader of her people, and will, with her brothers Moses and Aaron, form a sort of trinity in the great national epic.

What is more interesting, and more to the point in a book such as this, is that first "trinity" of which Miriam was a part: the Levite woman, the little girl, and the Egyptian princess. Three women, two cultures, reach across the great divide of power and religion to save an infant from death. It would not be an exaggeration to say that, without these women, the Exodus could never have taken place.

So it goes. Throughout much of history, women, though instrumental in ways great and small in the working out of human dilemmas, remain unheralded: their accomplishments overshadowed, their virtues belittled, their strength and constancy ignored. This is true in the Bible, and it is true in most standard histories of Western Christianity. Since the sixth century before the birth of Christ, when warrior kings evoked male sky gods and the age of the goddess crumbled, history has been written primarily by, about, and for men. What is finally being acknowledged now, as the second Christian millennium draws to a close, is that history was not necessarily made primarily by men. In every generation caring, dedicated, talented, vibrant women have contributed to the advancement of the human story, even though their own stories went untold.

In the pages of this book, you will meet four groups of women like this, women who lived their lives with a commitment that is admirable, and often died as a result. These women shared some things in common: a belief in Christianity, a steadfastness in the face of adversity, and a simplicity of life that somehow stirred up a disproportionate anxiety in ecclesiastical and civil authorities. They also lived in roughly the same areas: mainly the Low Countries, France, and Germany, as well as other states in western Europe.

The commonalities shared by these women, however, are balanced by the uniqueness of each group. The Beguines were laywomen who, for whatever reason, were unmarried. They found spiritual and material fulfillment in forming a new type of community without vows. The very "out-of-order" nature of their lifestyle, while it suited their needs and harmed no one, eventually made them the objects of suspicion and harassment by bishops and other clerics. The Anabaptists were part of the Radical Reformation, the second movement in the great religious upheavals of the sixteenth century. Together with the men of the movement, Anabaptist women immersed themselves in the scriptures and espoused a

Christianity so different that it threatened both Catholics and other Reformed Christians. The beliefs of the Anabaptists also set them at odds with civil authorities, and many of them paid the ultimate price, drowning in sacks or being burned at the stake.

The victims of the great witch hunts of the fifteenth through seventeenth centuries are perhaps the most unheralded and least understood of all the women in this book. There is no simple explanation for this horrendous phenomenon, just various theories about the who and the why. There is, sadly, no doubt about the how. Women—often old and poor, sometimes wealthy and independent—were rounded up, tortured, and finally burned to death, their ashes scattered to remove all trace of them from the earth. There is a seemingly endless number of books and countless articles about the European witch hunts. It is disheartening to realize that most of them are written by men, and most begin with the unexpressed assumption that these women were indeed "witches." Their story is gradually being reclaimed, as more openminded scholars attempt to retrieve the women behind the stereotypes.

Finally, the nuns of the monastery of Port-Royal in Paris found themselves caught up in the Jansenist controversy of the seventeenth and eighteenth centuries. That is another thread that binds these women together: they were all, in one form or another, accused of heresy, a lack of orthodox belief. In these pages, the Inquisition—the great ecclesiastical system designed to root out and punish heretics—plays a major and distressing role.

Like any 500-year period in the history of humanity, the period from the thirteenth to the eighteenth century in Western Europe is extraordinarily complex, filled with wars, sweeping economic and social changes, plagues, famines, and religious controversies. This book does not pretend to tell the whole story. Its purpose is simply to introduce the reader to four groups of women who thought themselves ordinary but who seem, on closer examination, quite amazing. Meeting them will, it is hoped, whet the reader's appetite to learn more about them and about the times in which they lived.

The Beguines. The Anabaptists. The so-called Witches. The Nuns of Port-Royal. They emerged in history unheralded and departed without ceremony. It is time to retrieve their memory and proclaim the good news of their devotion.

NOTES

1. George Arthur Buttrick, ed., *The Interpreter's Dictionary of the Bible* Volume 2 (New York: Abingdon Press, 1962), p. 582; *The Revell Bible Dictionary* (Grand Rapids, MI: Fleming H. Revell, 1990), pp. 481–482.

2. Phyllis Trible, "Bringing Miriam out of the Shadows," *Bible Review* (February 1989), pp. 16, 18.

Maps

Switzerland

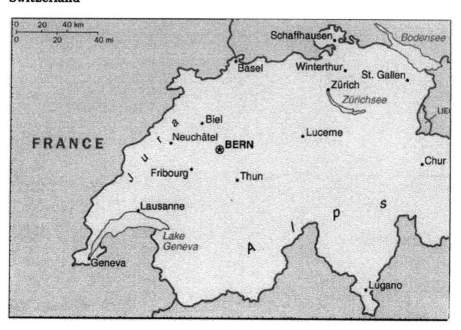

Belgium

France

Germany

Netherlands

xvii

1

The Thirteenth-Century Belgian Beguines: An Experiment in Laywomen's Spirituality

The beguines did not fit the ordinary pattern: they were women who were in the world, but not really part of it; pious women whose devotional ardor often surpassed that of cloistered nuns. Like them they dedicated their lives to God in a disciplined lifestyle, but unlike them they were not professed religious. In sum, it was the lifestyle of the early beguines, a lifestyle founded on intense spirituality, which differentiated them on the one hand from other laywomen and on the other from nuns.[1]

PROLOGUE

It is no secret that most congregations of women religious in the United States are having serious problems attracting and retaining new members. The median age of women religious rises with every passing year,[2] and many congregations have already recognized the need to reorganize, to merge with other groups, or to prepare for extinction.

There is no simple explanation for the demise of vocations to traditional religious life. No doubt, the obvious need to reinterpret the vows, especially poverty and obedience, in light of late-twentieth-century realities is one factor. Hard questions must be asked about the validity of claiming to be professionally poor while at the same time being surrounded by all the trappings of middle-class comfort. Obedience, too, must be reinterpreted in an age when so many religious choose their own jobs.

Beyond that, however, it is also true that today's young women are increasingly aware of both the possibility and the advantages of serving God and working for the church without joining a formal religious institution.

While many will see this as just the latest moment of decision in the history of individual institutes, others may recognize a *kairos*, a "sign of the times," if you will, a moment of opportunity, a call to change.

Another such moment, several centuries ago, gave birth to a form of lay spirituality that flourished, particularly in Flanders (modern-day Belgium) and the Netherlands in the twelfth and thirteenth centuries: the beguinages. Perhaps the beguines have something to say to today's religious and laywomen of all parts of society who are seeking to integrate the spiritual and material sides of life.

INTRODUCTION

In the northwest corner of Belgium, not so very far from the diamonds of Antwerp, the international business centers of Brussels, and the flowers of Ghent, lies the small medieval city of Brugge. Here, visitors can leave behind the psychological and physical overload that is modern Western life and be drawn into the pace of a simpler, if harsher, time.

Built on canals, Brugge is a collection of cobblestone streets that meander at odd angles and imitate the serpentine flow of the water. Even tourists living out their own "if it's Tuesday this must be Belgium" adventures find themselves slowing down, adapting to the pace of another era. Nor does Brugge allow such efforts to go unrewarded: around every curve, at every bend in the river, scenes unfold like living postcards. Inside every shop, overflowing with Belgian lace or Belgian chocolates or Belgian tapestries or even Belgian waffles, the people of Brugge add a warmth and a welcome that make lingering pleasurable and the thought of moving on distinctly distasteful.

In one beautiful corner of Brugge, near the *Minnewater* (Lake of Love) with its mascot swans, the visitor crosses a stone bridge with three arches and passes through an astonishingly beautiful gate. Americans have a special reason to pause here: the gate is dated 1776 and carries the words *Sauve/Garde*,[3] a symbolic offer of refuge from tyrannies of any kind. Once through the gate, the visitor enters a world of reverence, silence, peace, and serenity. This is the "the Vineyard," the *Begijnhof,* the Beguinage of Brugge.

HISTORICAL CONTEXT

To understand the beguines, it is necessary to understand the ecclesiastical and social background from which they emerged, for the origins of the beguinages are rooted in the complex and intertwined worlds of medieval feudalism, monasticism, and the papacy.

Socially, a tremendous transformation which fundamentally changed medieval Europe can be traced to a largely unexplained but nevertheless substantial increase in a population which had been stagnant or declining since the end of the Roman Empire. Beginning in the eleventh and twelfth centuries, urban life was reborn and historians note a new consciousness, an awareness of the place of Western Europe and Latin Christianity in the history of the world.[4]

The change resulting from this new consciousness was so extreme that Marc Bloch placed a line at 1050 CE and declared there were, in effect, two successive "feudal ages." The population growth of the second age drew groups of people together in the newly revitalized cities and called for a spiritual response as people tried to reconcile new economic and social realities with traditional religious doctrine.[5]

Prior to the eleventh century, European monasteries were becoming important social institutions. Most monks belonged to the nobility, and monastic poverty existed amid vast landholdings and agricultural enterprises. Monasteries were, for all practical purposes, part of the feudal system, with abbots who behaved like vassals of the king.[6] At the same time, the prestige of the popes was diminishing while rulers like Pepin (d.768) and Charlemagne (d.814) assumed the role of ecclesiastical leadership.

In the early ninth century, the Council of Aachen had decreed that every canonry had to provide a hospice for travelers, some sort of asylum for the poor, the unfortunate, virgins and widows, and have a hospital, and an orphanage. The cannonesses following the rule of Augustine made such charity a special part of their vocation. "Thus a continuum of ill-assorted women consistently irritated the orderly minds of early medieval reformers, a spiritual matrilineage for the Beguines, middle- and lower-class women pursuing religious life outside the convent, who emerge so dramatically in thirteenth-century sources."[7]

The late eleventh century saw the emergence of what has come to be called the Gregorian Reform. Gregory VII (d.1085) sought to free the church from outside political control and to restore papal authority. He decreed the pope had supreme power over all Christians. All prelates were subject to the pope, whose powers of absolution and excommunication were absolute. The Roman Curia was established as the central organ of church government. As a result, canon law and legal decrees, rather than the gospels, became the basis for moral judgement while the sacraments became increasingly legalistic.[8]

The eleventh-century reformers displayed considerable fear of and perhaps even hatred for women, leading to the final separation of the laity, and particularly women, from the priesthood. "The reformers were the first to articulate the *Frauenfrage*, the question of 'surplus' women, which came to be called the *cura mulierum* (the care of women), the clergyman's burden."[9]

In 1234 Gregory IX (d.1241) commissioned the Dominican Raymond of Peñafort to collect systematically the constitutions enacted by previous popes and councils, a codification of canon law published as *The Five Books of Decretals*. Now the church had a solidly hierarchical structure with supreme power vested in the pope. The only duty of both laity and religious was to obey. Popes, who were now elected by the cardinals, would not just be consecrated but crowned with a tiara, the sign of imperial power.[10] Bishops took a vow of obedience that sounded very much like the feudal oath of vassals.

At the same time other reformers within the church were seeking to purify the monasteries and put an end to unwarranted practices but without centralizing supreme power in the office and the person of the pope. The eleventh and twelfth centuries saw an amazing and widespread outbreak of lay spirituality throughout Europe, particularly in the northern countries. Men and women felt an intense fervor which could not be satisfied by existing ecclesiastical structures. They sought both to proclaim and to live out the gospel lifestyle, the *vita apostolica*.[11] In doing so, these Christians were seeking new ways to penetrate the world, unlike clerics and monastics who had withdrawn from it. This dual approach of returning to the gospel while remaining in the world guaranteed a Christian presence in society.[12]

The new role of the laity was a logical and necessary outcome of the revolution in progress. Since the evangelical awakening took place not by a revision of existing institutions but by a return to the gospel that bypassed these institutions, one could predict what its dynamics had to be: witness to the faith, fraternal love, poverty, the beatitudes—all these were to operate more spontaneously and sooner among laymen than among clerics, who were bound within an institutional framework.[13]

As towns grew, small communities of devout people too keen on freedom to take vows appeared. They devoted themselves to good works but outside the traditional ecclesiastical framework which raised practical problems for the church, especially in the areas of pastoral care and economic upkeep.[14]

THE BEGUINES

In the thirteenth century, church structures were increasingly inaccessible to women; convents were overcrowded and entrance dowries were expensive; women's orders were scarce and subject to male oversight. At this time in Liège and Antwerp, on the peripheries of urban centers, self-supporting communities of women began to appear. They lived by the work of their hands, often caring for the poor, the sick and the dying, and carried on regular devotional practices. They sought "an unstructured, nonhierarchical spiritual life that was both active (in the sense of ministering to the needs of others) and contemplative (in the sense that meditation and visionary experience were highly valued and developed)."[15] This was the seed of what would become the beguinages.

Groups of women outside convents, like the beguines, had to steer a narrow course in order to avoid "the shoals of anti-clericalism and heresy that always threatened the spiritual creativity of women."[16] The success and spread of the beguine movement would suggest it did answer a need felt among women for an independent expression of their own religious creativity.[17]

The beguines fall under the more general designation of *mulieres religiosae* (religious women), an umbrella term which included nuns, recluses, and virgins living at home or in small groups. The appearance of the *mulieres religiosae*, who flourished in the twelfth and thirteenth centuries, was a major religious development, possibly connected with factors like the Crusades, priestly celibacy,[18] and harsh physical labor, which resulted in women outnumbering men in Western Europe. Religious motives, however, were perhaps even more important than socio-economic ones.[19]

According to some authors, the beguines represent the first identifiable women's movement in Christianity.[20] The movement cannot be traced to any one individual or to any single foundation. It was part of the tendency of twelfth-century spirituality that increasingly absorbed facets of religious life into the lives of laypeople.[21] Women were looking for new ways to participate in the life of the church. Many women, while not called to or suited for the monastery, wanted to explore the religious meaning of their own everyday lives. Bypassing the very clerical authority by which they perhaps felt neglected or ignored, women tended to emphasize the human Christ, the affective approach to spirituality, and an integration of the gospel into the life of the society.[22] The religious life of the primitive church, with its poverty and humility, became the ideal;[23] evangelical poverty, with its common life and manual labor, was the guiding force.[24] "Voluntary poverty and the manual work associated with it were perhaps the key ingredients of the apostolic program of devout lay people who, forbidden by canon law to preach, were necessarily limited in their ability to save souls and imitate the lifestyle they associated with the primitive church."[25]

The beguine was a new creature, living in a pious community but free to leave at any time; not answerable to any man; self-determined and self-supporting. The lifestyle of the beguines was, perhaps, the "first respectable alternative to binding monastic vows or marriage."[26] Beguines may have been "part of a monolithic change in the lives of medieval women, a renewed impetus toward participation and leadership in public life."[27] "Where the reformed Benedictine system increasingly linked male houses together, women were more apt to maintain ties with friends and family, to depend for their support on the immediate neighborhood, and to direct their pastoral impulses to local needs."[28]

Scholars trace the development of the beguine movement through several stages, beginning with individual women (*beguinae singulariter in saeculo manentes*) living in towns but observing the evangelical principles as well as they could. These individuals eventually came together in the beguinages (*congregationes beguinarum disciplinatarum*) that are the main focus of this chapter. Later, some of the communities took the form of cloistered communities (*beguinae clausae*); finally, some communities were reconstituted as autonomous parishes.[29]

Far from withdrawing from the world, the beguines combined the freedom of lay people with the rules of religious orders. Although not bound by the three vows, the beguines paralleled groups like the Franciscans in their attempts to recover the simplicity of the early Christian communities.[30] Beguines joined together to devote themselves to prayer and good works, without removing themselves from "the world." "The twelfth-century religious awakening was marked by movement into the world, not withdrawal from it."[31] They retained their personal property and were free to leave the beguinage when and if they chose to do so.[32]

Although the origin of the term "beguine" remains a mystery,[33] by the thirteenth century the term was being applied generally to women who lived a quasi-religious life outside ecclesiastical jurisdiction.[34] These women were determined to live a life of prayer combined with charitable works, taking their biblical cue from the mission of the seventy in Luke, rather than the call to communal life in Acts.[35]

LIFESTYLE AND THEOLOGY

The development of the beguinages, however, while demonstrably an outgrowth of the lay religious awakening of the twelfth and thirteenth centuries, also reflected the social background of the era. Although much more positive than simply a stand against clerical mediocrity and Western feudalism, the growth of the beguinages did, nevertheless, provide alternatives to both. The beguinages represented a new way of giving religious significance to women's ordinary lives.[36]

It was characteristic of the beguinage to combine the *vita contemplativa* and appropriate devotional exercises with the practical solution of daily problems. The beguines customarily engaged in weaving, spinning, carding, charitable activity, sewing, and the education of children. So religious impetus and economic factors were intertwined in a beguine's life.[37]

Theologically, medieval women were faced with contradictory doctrines which placed them either on a pedestal or in a bottomless pit: the virgin or the temptress.[38] In the Christian view of sacred history, the greatest source of blessing for humanity after Christ was his mother, Mary; the greatest source of grief was also a woman, Eve, the mother of us all. So Christian tradition saw women as both the greatest and the weakest.[39]

Furthermore, while an astonishing variety of new male religious orders had begun to appear at the beginning of the twelfth century, there was no parallel development for women.[40] Women were advised to attach themselves to existing male orders but these orders were often either unable or unwilling to receive them. The Cistercians, for example, found it difficult to discipline the independent women who came to their monasteries.[41] Eventually "double monasteries" were suppressed, and women found other ways to satisfy their spiritual needs.[42] So the beguine movement emerged just as women's monastic activity was being restricted to cloistered contemplation. "Both the Premonstratensians[43] and medieval society at large were fundamentally intolerant of women who eluded men's direct control. Yet women still managed to express their piety in roles of chastity and charity throughout the Middle Ages."[44]

By shaping their own religious experience in lay communities, where female charisms served as as alternative to the male emphasis on the power of office, the beguines paralleled other women who were emerging from the feudal system and becoming economically independent through small crafts, shops, and businesses in new towns.[45] It has been suggested that the strength of the beguines lay in their unique combination of traditional spirituality with their freedom from the restrictions of the cloister, a combination which allowed them to experiment and break new ground.[46] Beguines adopted a chaste way of life and dressed simply, but they were not separated from the world, nor were they bound to any ecclesiastical authority.[47]

The beguine movement differed substantially from all earlier important movements within the western church. It was basically a women's movement, not simply a feminine appendix to a movement which owed its impetus, direction, and main support to men. It had no definite Rule of life; it claimed the authority of no saintly founder; it sought no authorization from the Holy See; it had no organization or constitution; it promised no benefits and sought no patrons; its vows were a statement of intention, not an irreversible commitment to a discipline enforced by authority; and its adherents could continue their ordinary work in the world.[48]

The beguine movement was essentially urban in character. Voluntarily embracing apostolic poverty, the women worked to support themselves and, in so doing, also met many of the needs of the new urban populations. It has been suggested that women like the beguines were largely responsible for a shift in the style of medieval piety. Their emphasis on caring for those in need, combined with a growing devotion to Mary, emphasized God's compassion and mercy in new ways. Some beguines dedicated themselves to the care of the sick, the laying out of the dead, and similar types of ministry, while others were involved in the weaving trade and other types of manual labor.[49] Beginning in the thirteenth century, hospitals and orphanages multiplied, witnessing to this new social consciousness.[50]

The fidelity of the beguines to their simple life of prayer and labor earned them high praise, even from some contemporary clerics. Robert Grosseteste, bishop of Lincoln, once noted that the beguines had achieved the highest degree of Christian perfection, while Robert de Sorbon remarked that the beguines might just give a better account of themselves than many a learned theologian.[51]

Beguines lived simply. Even those from wealthy families[52] lived on the income obtained by their own labor.[53] That labor, in turn, was itself one step away from the guild system which was developing during this same period. Guilds, or associations of merchants (merchant guilds) or artisans (craft guilds), were intended primarily to promote the interests of their members. The urban growth of the eleventh and twelfth centuries coincided with the initial flourishing of the guilds. Membership in a guild led to legal recognition and social permanence.[54] Under the guild system, women were shut out from independent access to the training and licensing needed for most skilled jobs; they were also paid half men's wages (since, it was presumed, they ate only half as much). Since the beguines did indeed live austerely they became, in a sense, the competitors of their male counterparts.[55] In fact, guilds sometimes objected to the beguines as unfair competition, since they were exempt from taxes.[56] So the beguines, although they were primarily prompted by spiritual motives, also became part of the answer to the *Frauenfrage*, the question of material provision for medieval women who, for whatever reason, were not married.[57] Some scholars recognize a parallel *Frauenbewegung* in the thirteenth and fourteenth centuries, a women's movement that saw an increased involvement by women in ministry, evangelism, guilds, and medical learning.[58] "By joining in beguinal communities, unattached urban women could pool their economic resources, find mutual protection, and gain a sense of identity."[59]

Joanna Ziegler points to two medieval documents that illuminate the double-pronged motivation (economic and religious) for entry into a beguinage. One, the general statutes for beguines in the diocese of Liège is addressed to "so many of you, virgins and women, who have been unable to find completely the access to obedience, or were able to do so without being able to bear the strictness of the Orders," who have chosen "wisely and prudently" to live a life of "virginity and modesty" in the company of "respectable and humble people." The other, a 1328 memorandum describes the beguines of St. Elisabeth's beguinage in Ghent as women who "because of their own condition and that of their friends, were shut off from a decent marriage," or, desiring to live in chastity "could not easily gain admittance to religious convents, owing to their multitude or to the poverty of their parents."[60] The beguinage at Brugge is typical of the Flemish or Walloon organization: a *curtis*, or enclosed complex of buildings, not unlike a New England village green[61] or a modern college campus which was actually a town within a town.[62] Little has described the Flemish beguinages as a successful strategy for avoiding the undesirable complexities of urban life while providing for homogeneous communities.[63] Each beguine had her own small house; an unusual feature of these houses in the beguinage at Brugge is the *cuisine à buffet*, an unusual kind of cupboard[64] where a meal could be prepared and eaten in total secrecy. In addition to the houses, other buildings in the complex accommodated beguinal activities: a church, an infirmary, and a weaving shop. So the beguinage was both a place of quiet solitude and a hub of activity. Although the beguinage was separated from the town by a wall, a canal, or joined houses. Brugge is an excellent example of this; the gate remained open all day and there was regular interaction between the beguines and the townsfolk.[65]

Although lacking any formal structure, and therefore essentially independent, beguines everywhere shared fundamental beliefs. There was a strong commitment to chastity. While beguines took no vow not to marry, those wishing to marry were expected to leave the community. Each beguinage had a head, or *Grootmeesteres*,[66] who was responsible for the orderly life of the group.

The beguines in general had no quarrel with orthodoxy nor did they introduce any distinctive theological ideas. They claimed no unique authority or revelation. They simply desired to life "religiously."[67] They were probably not even consciously protesting against the contemporary church. To reduce their motives to such negatives would disparage their positive goal of living a life suited to the Jesus of the gospels. Like many women of the period, the beguines seem to have had a special devotion to the Eucharist.[68]

SPIRITUALITY

What did the spirituality of the beguines look like? A scripture scholar once described spirituality as the particular way one group or individual organizes the various components of the Christian tradition, rather like storeowners arranging merchandise in shop windows.[69] If this is so, then beguine spirituality can best be described as Jesus-centered.

As part of the broader spiritual awakening of the twelfth and thirteenth centuries, the beguines took as their model the human Jesus, the itinerant preacher of the Synoptics, modeling their lives on his activities while on earth. The beguines' attraction to evangelical poverty exemplifies this.

Beguine spirituality also manifested the eucharistic fascination that was so much a part of medieval devotional life. Their devotion to the Passion was expressed through frequent mass and communion.

Beyond common prayer and liturgical exercises, however, beguine spirituality was also deeply interwoven with their insistence on manual labor. The Belgian beguines were known for their weaving and clothmaking, as well as for their nursing skills and their care for the poor. As Ziegler has pointed out, for beguines, "the hand was the primary tool that made the connection between the virtue expressed and the material manifestation of that virtue."[70] The beguines seemed to realize the ritual significance of tasks others might see as mindless and menial: sweeping floors, kneading bread, and so on.

Beguine Home, Beguinage, Brugges, Belgium.
Private collection.

Beguine Home—Mother Superior, Beguinage, Brugges, Belgium.
Private collection.

Bridge and Main Entrance, Brugges.
Private collection.

Schapraai (Cupboard), Brugges. Private
collection.

Two contemporary writers have offered their own suggestions about what was central to beguine spirituality. Ziegler sees the beguine communities of Belgium as one of the first, and perhaps most important audiences for the emerging sculptural program, the Pietà.[71]

There is much that is attractive about Ziegler's vision. The sculptural depiction of the dead Jesus in the arms of his mother would have had a magnetic appeal to women whose primary focus was the *imitatio Christi*. Although not found in any scriptural passage, the moment between the cross and the tomb cries out for a last maternal embrace. Furthermore, a sculpture, by its very nature, appeals to the tactile sense in a way no other art form does.

Ziegler contends that, for the beguines, spirituality was not a question of "transcending the reality of the senses," as it was for the better known women mystics of the period. For the beguines spiritual experience flowed from and included a sense of inner, intimate connection with material reality. Beguines "felt," in every sense of the word, the moment of encounter between dead son and grieving mother.[72]

Barbara Newman, for her part, sees a connection between the beguines and the literary form, *la mystique courtoise* (courtly love),[73] a new movement which Newman sees as both religious and literary.

Newman's hypothesis, based on the writings of medieval mystics who were beguines, may be more narrowly focused than that of Ziegler who looked at the communities of "ordinary" beguines, but it does emphasize the beguines as women of their day. Newman finds in the writings of the mystics and in the rule of at least one beguine community a startling synthesis of *eros* and *agape*, physical and spiritual love.[74]

A spirituality based on *la mystique courtoise* would naturally look at Jesus' great commandments of love. This in turn led to a particular devotion to the Sacred Heart, an image rapidly gaining in popularity during this period.[75]

One aspect of *la mystique courtoise* that is critical to this way of understanding beguine spirituality is the emphasis on community: "ecstasy finds its locus in community, and spiritual friends must be fiercely cherished."[76] In beguinages like that of Brugge, the physical layout delineated the varying degrees of intimacy among the beguines, and between the beguines and the wider society. While beguines primarily related to one another in a private, serene setting apart from the town, the bridge and gate allowed exchanges between the inner circle and the townspeople, albeit on the beguines' terms.

Both Ziegler and Newman have something important to say about beguine spirituality. Whether embodied in Ziegler's Pietà or Newman's courtly love, it seems apparent that the devotional life of the beguines was rooted in the broader cultural context of their day. They absorbed and then internalized emerging realities, making them uniquely their own. In doing so, they created a pattern of feminine spirituality that met their needs and still speaks to us today.

Beguine spirituality was rooted in the desire to imitate the Jesus of the Synoptics and was energized by a deep devotion to the Eucharist. This spirituality expressed itself in the daily combination of prayer and manual labor, and was enriched by new devotional icons that appealed to the tactile senses, like the Pietà, or to the literary senses, like courtly love and the Sacred Heart.

BEGUINE WRITINGS

Beguine spirituality integrated doctrine with spiritual experience. Devoting themselves to the poor and the sick, beguines seemed to reflect a joyous spirituality. Some beguines aspired to ecstatic religious experiences which led to the development of an intense mysticism. This in turn affected both religious and literary history. The earliest mystical writings in the northern European vernaculars were produced by beguines. In a period when the "vulgar" tongues were being emancipated, beguines were among those who studied and wrote about sacred themes and texts.[77]

Monica Furlong has described the twelfth to fifteenth centuries as a time when women were beginning to "stretch the boundaries of the confinement forced on the collective Eve."[78] Furlong sees the beguines as among the most striking innovators since they combined individuality with a sisterhood based on equality rather than hierarchy. The beguines "shadowed forth a wisdom that a triumphant church had mislaid."[79]

Many individual beguines wrote mystical treatises, poetry, or works reflecting the courtly love themes of secular literature. Beatrijs of Nazareth,[80] Mechthild of Magdeburg, and Hadewijch of Brabant were fascinated by the poetry of courtly love and adapted the language of the *minnesänger* and his lady to the soul longing for God.[81]

"Perhaps the greatest contribution of the women associated with the beguine movement is to be found in their writings, for it is there that they explored the experience of both human and divine life in new and unforgettable ways."[82] Beguine writers did what women had rarely done, namely, described their inner experiences of love and desire. "Love must be learned through relationship, and in the representation of such a relationship we see the discovery of the woman, the mother in god, and the god(dess) in the woman."[83]

Petroff sees shared beliefs in writings attributed to beguines: the nature of desire as both satisfying and painful; love as *jouissance*, or boundaryless sexuality; the indistinguishability of masculine and feminine; and a wholistic vision of body, soul, and heart.[84] The writings of mystical beguines may have influenced the thought of major mystical theorists like Meister Eckhart and Ruysbroeck. Beguinal writings are among the very few that describe mystical experiences from the point of view of those who really had them, and thus they provide valuable documentation for understanding actual mystical experiences.[85]

Like all medieval women, of course, beguines were excluded from the literary canon. Furthermore, since beguines did not fall under direct church supervision, "their religious enthusiasm and their prophetic gifts seldom received official approbation from the ecclesiastical hierarchy; they were often mocked for excessive piety and viewed with skepticism."[86]

More ominously, beguines were characterized as espousing unacceptable beliefs such as antinomianism which claimed that Christians have been freed by grace from observing the moral law.[87] "The Beguines were accused of antinomian heresies—it was very possible to interpret their writings as saying that if you had love you did not need to bother about virtue, even though what they were actually saying was that if you had love, virtue followed naturally."[88]

MARGUERITE PORETE AND THE INQUISITION

One beguine who paid the ultimate price for her writing was Marguerite Porete, also known as Margarita de Hannonia, indicating her birthplace in Hainaut, an area south of Flanders.[89] Marguerite was apparently well-educated; one account describes her as a "beguine capable in theology."[90] Toward the end of the thirteenth century, Marguerite published a book called *The Mirror of Simple Souls*. Written in Old French, *The Mirror* was a literary and mystical treatise that joined religious themes with the language of courtly love. The main speakers in *The Mirror* are Love, Reason, and the Soul. Marguerite used lively imagery, such as describing the liberated soul as the parchment on which the Spirit writes her message.[91]

The Mirror offers a frank treatment of mystical union and describes the true church as the community of the spiritually elite, superior to the "little church" governed by reason. Marguerite also refused to apologize for being a woman. "*The Mirror of Simple Souls* contains no hint of the conventional female apology for trespassing male terrain in writing about the highest things."[92] *The Mirror* makes no appeal to an authenticating visionary experience, claiming "the soul's annihilation in divinity is more valuable than the vision of the Trinity granted to St. Paul in the third heaven."[93]

At the heart of Marguerite's theology was the idea that the soul could be "annihilated" in a state of such union with God that it no longer had a separate existence. Since this view seems to circumvent church authority as obsolete, and to suggest that the annihilated soul could attain a sinless state without acts of penance and virtue, Marguerite's book posed a threat and a challenge to established ecclesiastical hierarchy and to the vowed religious life.[94] It opened her to charges of antinomianism and, between 1296 and 1306, Guy II, bishop of Cambrai, condemned *The Mirror of Simple Souls* and burned it at Valenciennes in Marguerite's presence.[95]

In April 1310, Marguerite faced the power of the inquisition in a series of consultations. She and her defender, Guiard de Cressonessart, had refused to take the oath required by the inquisition; both were imprisoned and excommunicated for eighteen months.[96] The threat of death worked on Guiard but not on Marguerite. At the second consultation, Guiard confessed and was declared a heretic because he held a theory of two churches and did not recognize the total supremacy of the pope in the universal church.

On April 11, 1310, twenty-one theologians condemned Marguerite's book as heretical. Such a large voice was deemed necessary since three theologians, at least one of whom was well known and respected, had previously approved the work. On May 9, Marguerite again refused to take the oath or to respond to the inquisitor's questions; she had also apparently ignored the bishop of Cambrai's injunction forbidding her to speak of her book. Consequently, it was decided that she deserved to be condemned as a heretic and to be turned over to the secular authorities. On May 31, she and Guiard were officially condemned. Guiard, who had recanted, was imprisoned for life; Marguerite was burned at the stake in the Place de Bièye, Paris, on June 1, 1310. Her condemnation referred to her as a *pseudo-mulier,* a relapsed heretic who had written a book filled with errors and heresies.[97]

Babinsky speculates about the real cause of Marguerite's death. Perhaps she was executed to demonstrate the absolute control of the inquisition over doctrine and discipline. Perhaps it was hoped that her death would tap into the suspicions of some Franciscans and Dominicans about the beguines, thus getting the support of the mendicant orders for other actions of the inquisition.[98] Perhaps Marguerite and Guiard were simply caught up in state-church politics and became symbols of some threat to royal and/or ecclesiastical power. Apparently Marguerite's book was quite popular, so there is also the possibility that her condemnation was meant as a warning to others who might be tempted to embrace new and "dangerous" theological views.

ECCLESIASTICAL DISAPPROVAL

The beguines were "extra-regular," that is, they were laywomen living together but not under the direct control of the hierarchy. The very independence that marked their emergence, however, eventually led to their decline. They were an anomaly; institutions like the church and medieval society had little time for anomalies. They made ecclesiastical authorities increasingly nervous because they belonged to no established order and followed no officially recognized rule.[99] The beguines exemplified the truth that a "religious" way of life is not dependent on institutional norms. They proved that women did not have to live in convents bound by three vows to lead a religious life.

The beguinage was a retreat, especially well-adapted to an urban society where women living in common could pursue chastity without a vow and earn a livelihood by suitable work. The life satisfied those who wanted to live religiously without severing all ties to the secular world.[100] But it also threatened some in positions of authority. "The beguines' awkward, middling posture produced a constant and finally destructive tension between themselves and thirteenth-century society, which had little sympathy for anomalous persons."[101] Women like the beguines violated the frontier between religious and secular individuals.

Beguines were essentially "out of order," outside, or at least between, fixed categories. As such, they challenged cultural and social assumptions; they did not "fit" into any of society's accepted female frames of social reference (religious, wife, widow, virgin), and yet they were somehow all of these.[102] "Beguines were urban culture's everywoman, the one who, for any number of reasons having to do with health, age, social status, physical deformity, or even freedom of choice, threatened to escape the predetermined social categories for women in the urban order."[103]

Herbert Grundmann has proposed that any analysis of beguine development—and decline—must be studied within the context of the relation of the religious women's movement as a whole to the papacy. The papal view held that all authentic religious life had to bound to particular regulations and established orders, that rules, norms, and discipline were essential in order to avoid error.[104] The Fourth Lateran Council in 1215 had forbidden the formation of any new religious orders; women could be treated only as annexes to existing male orders. The fact that beguines were "extra-regular" made them subject to suspicion and invective. William St. Amour, for example, who had been reprimanded by Rome for his attacks on the mendicant orders, turned his attention to the beguines, saying that, since they were violating church order, they ought to be excommunicated.[105] Other charges levied against the beguines included an overly close relationship with the Dominicans and the lack of oversight in the area of chastity. The mandate of the Council of Lyons in 1274 that any orders founded since 1215 without papal approval should be dissolved may have been directed at the beguines.[106]

The major attack against the beguines, however, surfaced at the Council of Vienne (1311–1312), which issued two decrees aimed at the women. *Cum de quibusdam mulieribus* (Concerning certain women)[107] condemned the status of beguines as being in violation of the Fourth Lateran Council's 1215 ban on new orders and accused the beguines of "madness" (presumably the "madness" was the Free Spirit heresy).[108] The decree did, however, observe that truly pious women could continue to live together. This was problematic since there were no clear criteria to separate the pious from the impious. *Ad Nostrum* outlined eight errors of "an abominable sect of malignant men known as beghards and faithless women known as beguines."[109] The errors were, in fact, the basic tenets of the movement known as the Free Spirit.

Briefly stated, these errors hold that: (1) humans can attain a sinless state; (2) in which sensuality is so subordinated to the soul that the body may be freely granted whatever it likes; (3) in this "spirit of liberty" individuals are not subject to human obedience; (4) and can attain the same perfection of beatitude on earth as in heaven; (5) every intelligent nature is blessed in itself; (6) and the acts of virtue are necessary only for those who are imperfect, for the perfect soul no longer needs to practice them; (7) the carnal act is not a sin; (8) the perfect should not rise during the elevation of the host, for to think of the sacrament of the Eucharist or the Passion of Christ would be a sign of imperfection.[110]

According to Bryant, the bull reflects the papacy's desire to legislate against heterodoxy. "The *Ad Nostrum*, which has been called a birth certificate without a baby, asserts that the Free Spirit abounded among the Beguines and Beghards."[111] This assumption is inaccurate. Not all beguines were Free Spirits, nor was the Free Spirit itself a discrete sect with organized members. It was a movement among the prosperous, literate classes in urban centers and middle-sized towns who were motivated more by a sincere search for spiritual perfection than by an anticlerical antagonism.[112]

Free Spirits sought to lead an uncompromisingly moral and holy life which, through arduous asceticism, would lead to union with God. "Free Spirits were mystics of different persuasions who appeared in different times and places and were related primarily by the circumstance that their mysticism was regarded as dangerous or unsound by ecclesiastical authorities."[113]

So *Ad Nostrum* was doubly wrong, treating both the beguines and the beghards[114] on the one hand, and the Free Spirit adherents on the other, as organized sects, an error Babinsky describes as "catastrophic." Thus, the greatest threat to the beguines came not from the heretical tendencies of some individuals but from the ambiguity and inaccuracy of the decrees of the Council of Vienne.[115]

Negative legislation did not deter the beguines, but it did obscure their efforts and deny them institutional support. In spite of this situation, the beguines continued their work of hospitality and shelter for travelers, as well as their care of the sick and the poor.

Further, although *Cum de quibusdam mulieribus* could be read as prohibiting and disbanding beguinal houses, its ambiguous language did not lead to a wholesale closing of the beguinages. In his bull *Racio recta* of 1318, John XXII tried to clarify matters by distinguishing between "good" and "bad" beguines, but even this document allowed broad local discretion. In 1343 Clement VI published a bull in which he declared he neither approved nor disapproved of the beguine lifestyle. So, by the fifteenth century there was a papal policy of toleration for the beguinal movement, but by then the movement had lost much of its early spontaneity.

CONCLUSION

The beguines were women of their day. They developed an integrated spirituality by drawing on all aspects of life—religious, social, artistic, and literary. This is, perhaps, the way in which beguine spirituality best provides a model for contemporary seekers.

In an age of spiritual awakening, when people from all walks of life desired to get closer to the human Jesus and live a more authentic gospel life, the beguines emerged as a uniquely woman's movement. Never wholly abandoning life "in the world," they nevertheless separated themselves from the increasingly materialistic goals that had come to characterize both church and society in the Middle Ages.

While not desirous of, or perhaps suited to, monastic life, these women met their own needs through the establishment of informal communities where they were free to pursue their spiritual goals while remaining actively involved in the life of the larger community.

If women today are seeking new ways to express their religious devotion—and the dramatic decrease in the number of those entering traditional convents would suggest this is so—they might do well to look to the beguines. The moment of *kairos* experienced by the women of the twelfth and thirteenth centuries is not unlike that challenging Christian women today who are still seeking ways to live according to gospel values in the midst of a materialistic and often skeptical world. The beguines stand ready, as always, to extend the hand of hospitality to visitors in need. Cross the bridge, enter the beguinage, and learn.

NOTES

1. Dennis Devlin, "Feminine Lay Piety in the High Middle Ages: The Beguines," in J. A. Nichols and L. T. Shank, eds., *Distant Echoes: Medieval Religious Women*, Volume One (Kalamazoo, MI: Cistercian Publications, 1984), p. 184.

2. The current median age is sixty-seven. The number of women religious in the United States has fallen from 1965's high of nearly 180,000 to 95,000 in 1993. In that year 460 women joined congregations while 3,000 either died or left. The current rate indicates that by the year 2000 there will be only 73,000. See also C. Bogert, "What If There Were None?" *Newsweek* (Dec. 26,1994/Jan. 2, 1995), p. 112.

3. "Save/Guard." "Beguinage" is the term used for the various living quarters of the beguines.

4. David Herlihy, *The Social History of Italy and Western Europe 700–1500: Collected Studies* (London: Various Reprints, 1979), p. 128.

5. Marc Bloch, "*La Société Féodale*," in Lester L. Little, *Religious Poverty and the Profit Economy in Medieval Europe* (Ithaca: Cornell University Press, 1978), pp. ix–x.

6. Richard P. McBrien, *Catholicism: Study Edition* (San Francisco: Harper & Row, 1981), p. 619.

7. Jo Ann Kay McNamara, *Sisters in Arms: Catholic Nuns through Two Millennia* (Cambridge, MA: Harvard University Press, 1996), pp. 205–206. McNamara sees some similarities between the canonesses and the beguines, perhaps suggesting a common origin: the right to earn money; the right to leave and marry; a semi-enclosed life; a common routine of prayer and work; and architecturally similar enclaves. She cites the satirical poet Rutebeuf: "Last year she wept; this year she prays; next year she will take a husband" (Rutebeuf, "*Li Dit des Beguines*," in Achile Jubinal, ed., *Oeuvres Complètes* [Paris: Bordas, 1874]).

8. McBrien, *Catholicism*, pp. 619–620. Three particular targets of Gregory's reform were simony (the buying and selling of ecclesiastical offices and spiritual goods); alienation (the passing of church property into the private hands of a bishop's or priest's offspring); and lay investiture (the practice of allowing lay lords to fill vacant bishoprics).

9. McNamara, *Sisters*, p. 220.

10. McBrien, *Catholicism*, p. 621. The tradition of crowning a pope continued until the consecration of Pope John Paul I in 1978. The *Decretals* remained in effect until 1917.

11. Brenda M. Bolton, "*Mulieres Sanctae*," in Derek Brown, ed., *Sanctity and Secularity: The Church and the World*, Studies in Church History, Volume 10 (New York: Barnes & Noble Books, 1973), p. 77.

12. Marie-Dominique Chenu, *Nature, Man, and Society in the Twelfth Century*, Jerome Taylor and Lester K. Little, eds./trans. (Chicago: University of Chicago Press, 1968), pp. 203, 238.

13. Chenu, *Nature*, p. 219.

14. Bolton, *Mulieres*, p. 77.

15. Elizabeth Alvilda Petroff, *Body and Soul: Essays on Medieval Women and Mysticism* (New York: Oxford University Press, 1994), pp. 51–52. Petroff notes that, while this was radical for its own day, it might, in fact, still appear radical today.

16. Jo Ann McNamara, "*De Quibusdam Mulieribus*: Reading Women's History from Hostile Sources," in Joel T. Rosenthal, ed., *Medieval Women and the Sources of Medieval History* (Athens: The University of Georgia Press, 1990), p. 237.

17. McNamara, "*De Quibusdam*," p. 238.

18. One of the targets of Gregory's reform, namely, alienation (the passing of church property into the private hands of a bishop's or a priest's offspring), helped pave the way for mandatory celibacy in the Western church. See McBrien, *Catholicism*, p. 619.

19. Roger DeGanck, *Beatrice of Nazareth in Her Context* (Kalamazoo, 1991), pp. 2–3.

20. See, for example, Caroline W. Bynum, *Holy Feast and Holy Fast: The Religious Significance of Food to Medieval Women* (Berkeley: University of California Press, 1987), p. 14.

21. Little, *Religious Poverty*, p. 129.

22. Bynum, *Holy Feast*, pp. 17–18.

23. Chenu, *Nature*, pp. 239–240. Chenu quotes Otto of Freising, *Chronica iv prol.*: "*Ego enim, ut de meo sensu loquar, utrum Deo magis placeat haec ecclesiae suae, quae nunc cernitur, exaltatio quam prior humiliatio, prorsus ignorare me profiteor. Videtur quidem status ille fuisse melior, iste felicior.*" ["Speaking frankly I do not really know whether the current prosperous condition of the church is more pleasing to God than its earlier humility. That earlier condition was perhaps better but the present is more agreeable."]

24. Devlin, "Feminine," p. 186.

25. Devlin, "Feminine," p. 188.

26. Carolly Erickson, *The Medieval Vision: Essays in History and Perception* (New York: Oxford University Press, 1976), p. 209.

27. Erickson, *Medieval Vision*, p. 210.

28. McNamara, *Sisters*, p. 206.

29. Little, *Religious Poverty*, p. 130. The "four-stage" theory of beguine development was first proposed by L.J.M. Philippen in *De Begijhoven, Oorsprong, Geschiedenis, Inrichting* (Antwerp: Veritas, 1918), and has been repeated by nearly all subsequent writers. In 1989, however, Walter Simons theorized that Philippen's pattern may be too organic. Curtis beguinages may have been simply a distinct form or option, not an outgrowth of the

isolated convent. See Walter Simons, "The Beguine Movement in the Southern Low Countries: A Reassessment," *Bulletin de l'Institut Historique Belge de Rome/Bulletin van het Belgisch Historisch Institut te Rome* 59 (1989): pp. 63–105.

30. Ernest W. McDonnell, *The Beguines and Beghards in Medieval Culture with Special Emphasis on the Belgian Scene* (New Brunswick, NJ: Rutgers University Press, 1954), pp. 1, 4–5.

31. Marguerite Porete, *The Mirror of Simple Souls*, Ellen L. Babinsky, trans./introduction (New York: Crossroad, 1993), p. 6.

32. Francine Prose, "Ancient Beguinages of Flanders," *The New York Times Magazine* (October 21, 1990), pp. 29, 44.

33. Suggestions include derivation from St. Beggar, daughter of Pepijn van Landen and an early patroness of the beguines (d.693); from Lambert de Begue (d.1177), a priest from Liège who was deeply interested in the popular religious movement; from *Albigensis*, or heretic, conveying ecclesiastical suspicion of popular piety; from the English "beg"; from the Old French word *beges*, meaning beige, the color of the beguines' dress; or even from the Middle Netherlands word, *bagga*, meaning "wearing thick clothes." See R. Hoornaert, *The Beguinage of Bruges: The Vineyard Then and Now*, P. A. Bennett, trans. (Ostend, 1988), p. 6. A Belgian legend holds that when Betrice, a Bohemian queen, was widowed, she and her two daughters, Ghiseldis and Nazarena, founded a community where they could live lives of simple piety. When others joined them, the group came to be called Beghina, using the initials of the three women. See Pierre Maes, "*Les Béguinages*," in *Tresors des Beguinages* (Ghent: Musée des Beaux Arts, 1961), p. 11.

34. Porete, *Mirror*, p. 7.

35. Luke 10:1–12; Acts: 4:32.

36. Bynum, *Holy Feast*, p. 17.

37. McDonnell, *Beguines*, p. 146.

38. E. Power, "The Position of Women," in C. G. Crump and E. F. Jacob, eds., *The Legacy of the Middle Ages* (Oxford: Oxford University Press, 1962), pp. 401–403.

39. Herlihy, *Social History*, p. 4. Herlihy's seventh chapter, "Alienation in Medieval Culture and Society," is a valuable resource for the social and economic factors influencing society as a whole during the Middle Ages.

40. Bolton, "*Mulieres*," p. 78.

41. The term "cistercian" is used to designate the Benedictine monks of Cîteaux (near Burgundy) who followed a strict observance, combining solitude and community, prayer and manual labor. They believed in simplicity in all things and were the first to demand uniformity among new monasteries, rather than the traditional autonomy. Carol Neel, in her article, "The Origin of the Beguines," in Judith M. Bennett, Elizabeth A. Clark, Jean F. O'Barr, Anne Vilen, and Sarah Westphal-Wihl, eds., *Sisters and Workers in the Middle Ages* (Chicago: University of Chicago Press, 1989), pp. 240–260, argues that the beguines might be more closely related to the women of Cîteaux and Prémontré than is usually supposed. She sees similarities between cistercian and beguine spirituality and notes that the

Premonstratensians encouraged piety among women of many levels of society. Further, she points out that the Flemish beguines were concentrated in the same geographical area as the Order of Prémontré.

42. See R. W. Southern, *Western Society and the Church in the Middle Ages*, The Pelican History of the Church, Volume Two (Baltimore: Penguin Books, 1973), pp. 312–318.

43. The term "Premonstratensian" refers to the Order of the Canons Regular of Prémontré. The order was founded by Norbert in 1120 and is sometimes called the Norbertines. They adopted the rule of Augustine with some variations. Since Norbert was friendly with Bernard of Clairvaux, the force behind the reform of Cîteaux, the Norbertines also exhibited some cistercian influence.

44. Neel, "Origin," p. 258.

45. Bynum, *Holy Feast*, p. 22.

46. Devlin, "Feminine," p. 189.

47. Florence Koorn, "Women without Vows: The Case of the Beguines and the Sisters of the Common Life in the Northern Netherlands," Anne MacLachlan, trans., in Elisja Schulte van Kessel, ed., *Women and Men in Spiritual Culture: XIV–XVII Centuries* (The Hague: Netherlands Government Publishing Office, 1984), p. 135.

48. Southern, *Western Society*, p. 321.

49. Emilie Zum Brunn and Georgette Epiney Burgard, *Women Mystics in Medieval Europe* (New York: Paragon House, 1989), p. xxi.

50. Herlihy, *Social History*, pp. 13–14. It was perhaps this involvement in the care of the sick and the dying that allowed the beguines of the Low Countries to survive the threatening periods of the Reformation and the French Revolution, since their work reinforced their nonmonastic status. Pierre Maes, "*Béguinages*," pp. 18–24.

51. Bolton, "*Mulieres*," p. 83. In another article, Bolton quotes Humbert de Romano, minister general of the Dominican Order: "*in medio peruersae nationis ducunt uitam sanctissimam. . . . Felices Beguinae. . . . laude dignissimae.*" ["Those happy beguines, most worthy of praise, who in the midst of a perverse generation are leading lives of the greatest sanctity."] See Brenda M. Bolton, "Some Thirteenth Century Women in the Low Countries: A Special Case?" *Nederlands Archief voor Kerkgeschiedenis* 61, 1 (1981): p. 7.

52. Earlier popular opinion placed the rise of movements such as the beguines among the lowest social strata, seeing such developments as a sort of social protest based on economic need. It can be demonstrated, however, that many, if not most, of the original beguines were, in fact, women of wealth and station, although membership eventually cut across all social and economic classes. See, for example, McDonnell, *Beguines*, pp. 81–82. McDonnell adds that many of the beguinages did become refuges for the poor, offering lodging and food to girls and widows.

53. DeGanck, *Beatrice*, pp. 24–25.

54. See Joseph Strayer, ed., *Dictionary of the Middle Ages*, Volume 6 (New York: Scribner, 1982), pp. 13–20, for a more extensive treatment of the history and development of the medieval guild system.

55. McNamara, *Sisters*, p. 283. McNamara later theorizes that the craftsmen equated economic aggressiveness with sexual agressiveness, an evocative link to the witch craze which will be discussed in chapter 3 of this book. McNamara, *Sisters*, p. 431.

56. Katharina M. Wilson, ed., *Medieval Women Writers* (Athens: University of Georgia Press, 1984), p. xv.

57. McDonnell, *Beguines*, pp. 83–84. There are many reasons cited for the relatively large number of unmarried women at this historical moment. Among the most commonly cited factors are wars; the Crusades; the greater longevity of women; monastic life; an increase in the "cost" of dowries for marriage or the monastery; and the guild system which prohibited apprentices from marrying until they attained masterhood. McDonnell also points out that women of aristocratic birth actually had fewer life choices than those of humbler origin. While artisans' daughters could be apprenticed and work in trades like the cloth industry, the daughters of the nobility could not; nor could they enter a marriage or a convent whose dowry was lower than that of their own rank. See McDonnell, p. 85. See also Prose, "Ancient Beguinages," p. 29.

58. Erickson, *Medieval Vision*, p. 208.

59. Robert E. Lerner, "Beguines and Beghards," in Joseph Strayer, ed., *Dictionary of the Middle Ages*, Volume 2 (New York: Scribner, 1982), p. 160.

60. Joanna E. Ziegler, *Sculpture of Compassion: The Pietà and the Beguines in the Southern Low Countries c.1300–c.1600* (Brussels: Institut historique belge de Rome, 1992), pp. 82–83. The documents are "The Statutes of the Beguine Communities in the Diocese of Liège," c. 1246, L.J.M. Phillipen, ed., *De Begijnhoven*, pp. 303–304; and "Memorandum Presented to the Delegates of the Bishop of Tournai in Favor of the Beguinage of Saint Elisabeth in Ghent," 1328, J. Béthune, ed., *Cartulaire du Béguinage de Sainte Elisabeth à Ghent* (Bruges: Aimé de Zuttere, 1883), p. 74.

61. Prose, "Ancient Beguinages," p. 29. Beguines thus were separated from the world, while keeping one foot firmly planted in it.

62. The *curtis* beguinage combined community with autonomy, and individual priorities with collective priorities. See Ziegler, *Sculpture*, p. 76.

63. Little, *Religious*, p. 131.

64. The cupboard, *Schapraai* in Flemish, was tall and narrow, with three doors opening into three compartments: the top held the crockery; the middle allowed meals to be prepared; the bottom held the provisions. A sliding board which formed a table separated the last two; this is where the beguine ate her meals.

65. Koorn, "Women," p. 139. There were, of course, prohibitions against meeting privately or dining with men.

66. Also *Grootjuffrouw*, "Great Lady."

67. Southern, *Western Society*, p. 322.

68. Medieval eucharistic devotion is beyond the scope of this article. In this connection see, for example, Caroline Walker Bynum, "Women Mystics and Eucharistic Devotion in the Thirteenth Century," *Women's Studies*, 11 (1984), pp. 179–214.

69. Addison Wright, SS, lecturer, Marywood University, Scranton, Pennsylvania.

70. Ziegler, *Sculpture*, p. 103.

71. This hypothesis is worked out in great detail in Ziegler's book, *Sculpture of Compassion*, cited above.

72. Ziegler, *Sculpture*, p. 113.

73. Barbara Newman, *From Virile Woman to Woman-Christ: Studies in Medieval Religion and Literature* (Philadelphia: University of Pennsylvania Press, 1995).

74. Newman, *Virile Woman*, p. 139. The rule is the *Règle des Fins Amans*, written by a French priest to articulate the ideals of the community.

75. Newman, *Virile Woman*, p. 141.

76. Newman, *Virile Woman*, p. 142.

77. Zum Brunn and Burgard, *Women Mystics*, pp. xiv–xv, xxii. The use of the "vulgar" languages, however, only served to increase hierarchical suspicion.

78. Monica Furlong, *Vision & Longings: Medieval Women Mystics* (Boston: Shambhala Publications, Inc., 1996), pp. 17–18.

79. Furlong, *Vision*, p. 38.

80. The first known mystical tract in a European vernacular was Beatrijs' Flemish *Seven Manieren von Minne* (*The Seven Manners of Love*).

81. Furlong, *Vision*, p. 104.

82. Petroff, *Body and Soul*, p. 56.

83. Petroff, *Body and Soul*, p. 56.

84. Petroff, *Body and Soul*, pp. 61–62.

85. Joseph R. Strayer, ed., *Dictionary of the Middle Ages* Volume 2 (New York: Charles Scribner's Sons, 1983), p. 160.

86. Wilson, *Medieval Women*, pp. vii, xiv.

87. This belief arose from a misinterpretation of Paul, whose emphasis on the gratuity of grace through faith in Christ rather than the efficacy of the Mosaic law was seen by some as a rejection of the need to observe the moral commandments.

88. Furlong, *Vision*, p. 104.

89. Amy Oden, *In Her Words: Women's Writings in the History of Christian Thought* (Nashville: Abingdon Press, 1994), p. 158.

90. The phrase is "*beghine en clefgie mutl suffissant*," found in Jean d'Outremeuse des Preis, *Myreur des Histors*, Volume 6, pp. 141–142, in Gwendolyn Bryant, "The French Heretic Marguerite Porete," in Wilson, *Medieval Women*, p. 204.

91. Porete, *Mirror*, pp. 1–2.

92. Moseh Idel and Bernard McGinn, *Mysticism and Monotheistic Faith: An Ecumenical Dialogue* (New York: Macmillan Publishing Co., 1989), cited by Robert E. Lerner in his Preface to Babinsky's translation of *Mirror*, p. 3.

93. Porete, *Mirror*, p. 3.

94. Oden, *In Her Words*, p. 159.

95. Bryant, "French Heretic," p. 204.

96. What follows draws heavily on Ellen Babinsky's introduction to her translation of Porete's *Mirror*, pp. 21–26.

97. Of the little that is known of Marguerite Porete, much comes from the inquisitorial records and the text of the execution. See Paul Verdeyen, "*Le Procès d'Inquisiton contre Marguerite Porete et Guiard de Cressonessart* (1309–1310)," *Revue d'Histoire Ecclésiastique* 81 (1986).

98. Babinsky makes an interesting case for placing Marguerite's trial and execution against the backdrop of the Templar controversy, but that is beyond the scope of this chapter.

99. DeGanck, *Beatrice*, p. 5.

100. McDonnell, *Beguines*, p. 131.

101. Neel, "Origin," p. 242.

102. Ziegler, *Sculpture*, p. 88.

103. Ziegler, *Sculpture*, p. 92.

104. Herbert Grundmann, *Religiöse Bewegungen im Mittelalter: Untersuchungen Über die Geschichtlichen Zusammenhange Zwischen der Ketzerei, 12. und 13. in Jahrhundert und die Geschichtlichen Grundiagen der Deutschen Mystik* (Berline, 1935), cited in Porete, *Mirror*, pp. 7–8.

105. William St. Amour may have been using his attacks on the beguines and beghards to further his campaign against the mendicant friars. He went so far as to characterize the beguines as "totally evil." See Strayer, *The Dictionary of the Middle Ages*, Volume 2, p. 159.

106. Porete, *Mirror*, pp. 9–10.

107. In answer to her own question, "Who were these 'certain women'?" Jo Ann McNamara responds that they were women "who attempted to be the center of their own lives and even to draw others around them. But [she warns] our sources reveal them only on the fringes of religious movements dominated by others. Their histories are fractured by hostile sources. This is the history we were all trained not to write: a history in confrontation with our sources rather than in conformity with them" (McNamara, "*De Quibusdam*," p. 239).

108. "Heresy" is a problematic term even today, and was used quite loosely in the Middle Ages. Herlihy points out that the Greek root indicates "to choose" rather than "to reject," that is, the person involved is positively selecting a belief and not primarily opposing official teaching. See Herlihy, *Social History*, pp. 128–129.

109. Porete, *Mirror*, p. 11.

110. This information is widely available. Here I am using Bryant, "The French Heretic," p. 207.

111. Bryant, "The French Heretic," p. 207.

112. See Robert E. Lerner, *The Heresy of the Free Spirit in the Late Middle Ages* (Los Angeles: University of California Press, 1972), pp. 85–163.

113. Joseph Strayer, ed., *Dictionary of the Middle Ages*, Volume 5, p. 216.

114. "Beghards" is the term used to refer to lay fraternities of men that arose in Flanders in the thirteenth century, contemporaneously with the beguines.

115. Porete, *Mirror*, p. 8.

2

Anabaptist Women Martyrs:
Images of Radical Commitment

The [women] letter writers mostly described their faith and hope. It was a faith requiring adult, conscious consent and discipleship and suffering along the pattern of Jesus and the early church. . . . The letters also reflect the writers' strong earthly bonds with spouses and children . . . , as they expressed their longing for the physical presence of their loved ones. These Anabaptists were convinced that their otherworldly expectations were absolutely accurate, but at the same time they unabashedly admit a hearty love for their families.[1]

PROLOGUE

One summer afternoon a few years ago, I went in search of martyrs. My pilgrimage was short and certain: from the campus of the University of Notre Dame in South Bend, Indiana, where I was doing doctoral studies in Theology, to the library of the Associated Mennonite Biblical Seminaries in nearby Elkhart. The library was the temporary home of an exhibit of copper plate etchings created by the Dutch artist Jan Luyken for the 1660 edition of Thieleman van Braght's *Martyrs' Mirror*,[2] an Anabaptist martyrology.

It was one of those spectacular summer days when the midwestern sky is the color of star sapphires and the plump, puffy clouds are as white as the cornfields after a February blizzard. Such a day is always welcome, but never more so than when it comes as it did then after a week of heat and high humidity.

The drive itself was an apt metaphor for the purpose of my solitary journey. As I drove east from South Bend the road was crowded with cars heading for the myriad discount stores, malls and shopping centers that dominate the area surrounding Notre Dame. Then I crossed Grape Road and entered an entirely different world. Gone were the fast food restaurants, the warehouse outlets, the array of car dealerships; in their place were modest homes with large lawns and acres of cornfields. Suddenly, too, I was alone, free to contemplate the contrast between the serene beauty of the day and the bloody violence into which I planned once again to immerse myself.

Martyrs' Mirror and the people whose lives and deaths it describes have had an almost magnetic attraction for me for several years, since the day I was first introduced to them. I was tempted to write "the *heroic* people," even though the Anabaptist martyrs did not think of themselves as heroic. They were ordinary simple people, with an extraordinarily simple view of Christianity: to be a Christian meant to follow the Christ of the gospels. Their ability to cut to the heart of Christian commitment, their willingness to get to the roots of the gospel message, caused them to be called radicals and to be hated and feared by Romans and Reformers alike. That, too, is part of their appeal. Even today, four centuries after the death of the last Anabaptist martyr,[3] these remarkable men and women still challenge the established churches to examine their understanding of what it means to be a Christian in a materialistic world.

It was, in fact, growing affluence and acculturation after nearly a century of tolerance that inspired some of the descendants of the original Anabaptists to gather the stories and letters of the sixteenth-century martyrs into a volume that could be read, shared and revered. In his preface, van Braght observes that to those who judge by externals, things are better in his day (the mid-1600s), since quiet and comfort prevail. But for those who look to spiritual values, he warns, the times are actually more dangerous than the days of the martyrs. In times of persecution Satan comes openly and can be easily recognized, but in times of affluence Satan assumes a pleasing form and souls are ruined before they are even aware of their danger.

The application to our own day is obvious. Before looking at what we modern Christians might see were we to gaze into the *Martyrs' Mirror*, however, I would like to go back and find out just what it was about these simple folk, these "Christ-minded ones," as they thought of themselves before others dubbed them Anabaptists ("doublebaptizers") that so threatened larger, more powerful and better organized church groups. What was it that moved the Romans, the Calvinists and others to persecute them so fiercely and to work so hard for their extinction?

HISTORICAL BACKGROUND

The abuses which led up to the Reformation are well documented, as are the various movements which claimed to have recaptured the spirit of early Christianity. Many of the more blatant of these abuses can be traced to the material flourishing of the church after the Constantinian settlement, a flourishing which led the church to adopt many of the externals of the ancient Roman Empire. By the twelfth century, the church's authority was virtually universal and unavoidable.

Some of the societal factors leading to the Reformation include the developing book culture, the waning of feudalism and the emergence of a monetary economy with merchants and artisans, the birth of new nations and a growing spirit of nationalism, new trade routes to the Far East, and, perhaps most importantly, the invention of the printing press. During this time, too, age-old assumptions about God and the universe were being questioned. It was, in short, a very unsettled and unsettling time.[4]

In addition to these societal factors, there were ecclesiastical issues, such as the papal schism[5] and the inquisition, an institution established after the Fourth Lateran Council in the thirteenth century to identify and eradicate heresies.[6]

After the schism . . . the papacy emerged as something between an Italian cityctate and a European power, without forgetting at the same time the claim to be the viceregent of Christ. The pope often could not make up his mind whether he was the successor of Peter or of Caesar. Such vacillation had much to do with the rise and success, not to mention the necessity, of the Reformation.[7]

An early reform movement in response to this decreased prestige of the papacy arose in Bohemia under the leadership of John Hus (c.1372–1415), who translated some of the writings of the English philosopher and theologian John Wyclif into Czech. Wyclif has been referred to as the "Morning Star of the Reformation." Convinced that the church should be as poor as the first disciples, and that it had only spiritual authority, Wyclif urged the king to reform the church, by force if necessary. Wyclif also believed that all people should have access to the scriptures. To that end, he trained preachers, called

"Lollards," who memorized long biblical passages and then wandered the countryside reciting them.[8]

Wyclif's calls for church reform had been condemned by the English synod and by Gregory XI in 1377. Wyclif claimed, among other things, that the state could lawfully deprive corrupt clergy of their endowments and that papal claims to temporal power had no biblical warrant. These ideas appealed to Hus who was a fierce critic of an immoral papacy and clergy. Hus developed a deeper understanding of the nature of the church which was found, he claimed, not where the pope was but where two or three were gathered in the name of Christ. It was the Holy Spirit, not the pope, who gave authority to the church. Hus was so effective that 105 years later Luther observed, "We are all Hussites without knowing it."[9]

Called to appear before the Council of Constance in 1415, Hus was promised safe conduct by Emperor Sigismund. Despite this assurance, Hus was condemned by the council and executed.

A century later, Luther would be compared to Hus. . . . Both Wyclif and Hus were signs of growing national consciousness and criticism of the church. After his execution, Hus was declared a martyr and national hero by the University of Prague. Hus's prophecy that though his enemies were burning a goose at the stake ("*Hus*" in Czech means "goose") a swan would follow that they could not burn was popularly applied to Luther.[10]

In 1572 a picture was painted in Bohemia showing Wyclif holding a spark, Hus kindling the coals with it, and Luther holding up the flaming torch.[11]

Another major factor leading up to the events of the sixteenth century was the launching of the Crusades, a series of wars beginning in the eleventh century, which were fought under the banner of Christ with the goal of the recovery of Christian lands. Although at first directed against Muslim expansion in Spain and Sicily, the Crusades' ultimate objective was the liberation of Jerusalem and the Holy Land. In their effort to attract soldiers, the popes offered indulgences, assurances that, having fought "before the cross," crusaders would, at the time of death, be freed of any temporal punishment due to sin.[12] Questionable even in its earlier, purer form, the practice of indulgences took on a decidedly materialistic tone during the Crusades. While crusaders were automatically granted plenary indulgences (the remission of all temporal punishment incurred by sin), the wealthy who could not or would not take part personally in the Crusades could share in the indulgence by financing the campaigns.[13] Many interested in reforming the church saw this as buying and selling salvation; this became one of the direct causes of Luther's 1517 protest.

Another source of growing dissatisfaction to many was the increasingly complex sacramental system. By the end of the Middle Ages the rituals surrounding the sacraments had become more important than the realities behind them. Pilgrimages and shrines, relics and miracles, replaced the gospels as the core of the simple Christian's religion. Cornelius Dyck has said it well:

The Reformation did not come unannounced, though the way in which it shook the foundations of Europe was unexpected. The influence of the Crusades and of the Renaissance, the rise of nationalism and its clash with the international papal church, the corruption of the clergy and the church, the growing restlessness of the common people all became signs that a major storm was about to break.[14]

Early reformers, people like Francis of Assisi, Peter Waldo,[15] and John Wyclif, sought to recapture the Jesus of the gospels and to imitate his life and spirituality. One key to all attempts at reform was the Bible. The scriptures had to be made available to all Christians, and the authority of those scriptures over that of the church, as Hus had claimed, had to be asserted.

Another major stepping stone on the way to the Reformation was the emergence of humanism and the humanists. Humanism was at the heart of the Renaissance, the fourteenth- and fifteenth-century recovery of the culture of ancient Greece and Rome. The period of humanism was marked above all by a new spirit of freedom and inquiry. It was the humanists who "rediscovered" the scriptures and gave a new impetus to biblical scholarship. One such humanist was Erasmus (1466–1536), the Dutch scholar, author, and critic. Although Erasmus remained a devout Catholic, and, in fact, opposed the Reformation, his influence on the early reformers was so pronounced that it has been said that Erasmus laid the egg which Luther hatched. Erasmus believed that true reform could be achieved through a humanist study of the Bible and the early patristic writings. In 1516 he published a Greek and Latin version of the New Testament in which he translated critical Greek terms differently from the standard medieval Vulgate edition. Because he was seen as a cause of the Reformation, Erasmus' works were placed on the Index of Forbidden Books,[16] but his influence was immense.[17]

Martin Luther (1483–1546) was born in Eisleben, Germany and educated in law. After a near-death experience he became an Augustinian priest and later earned a doctorate in theology at Wittenberg. It was as a professor of biblical studies at Wittenberg that

Luther first confronted many of his later issues. His arguments against indulgences, as well as his interpretation of grace and faith, threatened the sacramental system. This in turn led to a dispute over authority in the church. Luther's personal turning point came through his study of the Pauline letters: we are justified by faith in Christ, not by good works.

On the eve of All Saints Day in 1517 Luther posted his "Ninety-Five Theses" on the door of the church in Wittenberg. In disputations following his action, Luther denied papal infallibility and questioned canon law. When he was, in turn, asked the source of authority for his own views, he cited scripture alone.

Rome's attack on Luther antagonized Germany, where nationalists defended him and offered him asylum, if necessary. Renaissance humanists like Erasmus found much to admire in Luther's work, although after the publication of the German's, *The Babylonian Captivity*, Erasmus declared the breach irreparable.

Among Luther's supporters mass was celebrated in the vernacular and the cup, so long withheld from the laity, was restored. Priests, including eventually Luther himself, began to marry. But Luther was essentially conservative and before long other reformers would go to extremes he could not tolerate. At the same time attempts at reform were being made outside Germany. The leader of one of these attempts, Ulrich Zwingli of Zurich, set the stage for the emergence of the Anabaptists.

Not too many years after Luther began his reform in Germany, Ulrich Zwingli (1484–1531) became a predominant figure in the Swiss Reform movement. Zwingli was a priest who had been influenced by Erasmus. Called to be the People's Preacher at the Great Minster in Zurich, Switzerland, Zwingli roused the people with his attacks against the abuses of the Catholic Church. Supported by the city council, Zwingli implemented his vision, which included the Lord's Supper in German, sole reliance on scripture, the nullification of canon law, the removal of images and organs from churches, and the dissolution of monasteries. When, in 1522, Zwingli resigned as a Roman priest, the ruling body of Zurich, the Council of Two Hundred, immediately reinstated him. This was the beginning of the state church in Switzerland.

By 1523 the break with Rome had been finalized, a painful reality since Zwingli had been a priest and the council members had been Catholics. Zwingli's reform was more comprehensive than Luther's, perhaps because Zwingli had been trained as a systematic theologian. In 1525 Zwingli published his longest and most important work, *Of the True and False Religion*, the first systematic theology by a Protestant theologian. Zwingli saw no middle ground: whatever was wrong had to be discarded. So the Reformation took a more radical path in Switzerland than it had in Germany.[18]

While Zwingli was willing to allow the government to control the way in which reforms were implemented in Zurich, however, some of his followers grew impatient with the continued delays. Three in particular, Conrad Grebel, Simon Stumpf, and Wilhelm Reublin, began to question both the political organization of Zurich and the practice of infant baptism. At a 1523 theological debate on the issues facing the Zurich state church, Grebel expressed disappointment with Zwingli's reform. Grebel, the son of an upperclass Zurich family, had dallied in Vienna and Paris as a university student until Zwingli inspired in him a strong personal commitment to the gospel. At the debate, Grebel took issue with what he considered the unnecessary delay in abolishing the mass and argued against infant baptism.[19] Anabaptism thus arose "in Zwingli's own circle as the result of an effort to carry through more consistently the program of the restoration of primitive Christianity."[20] The early church had been composed only of true believers. It was not supported by the state but persecuted, a church of martyrs.

According to Dyck the first sign of these three men and their adherents as a self-conscious group can be found in three letters written by Grebel and his friends in September of 1524. These letters make it clear that the Word of God alone had authority for the true Christian and that the followers of Christ were not to look to the state for support or protection, even in the face of grave personal danger. Adult, or believers, baptism was embraced since baptism required a real commitment on the part of the one baptized. Although baptism was not the central issue for these people, it was the one that put them in direct conflict with the council of Zurich, which had decreed that infants should continue to be baptized. The penalty for parents who failed in this duty was expulsion from the city. This decree, in January of 1525, was a signal that force might be used against those who held religious views contrary to that of the majority.[21]

The real question was not the ritual of baptism but the way in which it functioned in the formation of the church. While others jeeringly began to refer to the new group as "Anabaptists,"[22] they saw themselves as adult believers who had sealed their belief in water and the Spirit. They formed a church that was as different from the other Reformed churches as it was from the medieval Roman church.

Unlike Luther, who objected to Rome's teachings, the Anabaptists rejected what they saw as Rome's lack of ethics and a moral lifestyle. They also complained that the reforms of Luther and Zwingli did not improve that lifestyle.[23] A famous quotation from an Anabaptist account of the origins of the sect observed that Luther "tore down the old house but built no new one in its place" and that Zwingli "threw down all infirmities as with thunder strokes, but erected nothing better in their place."[24]

Although they called themselves simply "Baptists," labeling them "Anabaptists" (rebaptizers) allowed Justinian's code to be used against them as it had been against the Donatists.[25] According to the *Codex Justinianus*, rebaptism was punishable by death. "The crime was a religious ritual, baptism received for a second time, but also the efect which stemmed from it, that of conflict and disunity within the empire."[26]

It would be naïve, however, to believe that opposition toward the Anabaptists sprang from purely religious or theological motives. Anabaptists called for the end of tithes and other ecclesiastical dues. Zwingli had spoken in favor of this reform but in the end supported the burghers who condemned the action in a resolution passed in June of 1523. This marked the parting of the ways for Zwingli and the new sect.

The decisive crisis was a debate in city council on October 26, 1523, during which Grebel denounced various matters connected with the Eucharist such as mixing wine with water, the use of unleavened bread, and distribution by a priest. Stumpf accused Zwingli of handing spiritual authority over to the civil leaders. The Anabaptists rejected this as substituting Swiss guildmasters for the Roman hierarchy. The Council sided with Zwingli and the break was complete.[27]

On January 21, 1525, Georg Blaurock asked Grebel for baptism. Consequently, this is the date usually cited as the beginning of formal Anabaptism. Josef von Beck described the pivotal event:

God hath called to this wonderful work men in Switzerland; amongst them have been Balthazar Hubmeyer, Konrad Grebel, Felix Manz, and Georg von Chur. These men have recognized that one must first of all learn the Divine message, the love of an active faith, and only after having done so, should he receive Christian baptism. But since, at that time, there was no servant ordained to such work, Georg of the house of Jacob called Blaurock rose up and prayed this Konrad Grebel in the name of God, that he should baptise him. After that was done, the others there present did demand the same from Georg, and began to hold and teach the faith. Therewith hath the separation from the world originated and hath grown up.[28]

The Anabaptist view of government reflected the basic dualism of their theology. While acknowledging that all governments, good or bad, were established by God, and thus had divine sanction, Anabaptists declared that the only reason for government was to keep sinful people from destroying each other. Therefore, governments had authority only in secular matters and faithful Christians were not bound by them.

As a result of this concept of government, most Anabaptists refused to carry or use weapons, pay war tithes, go to court, or swear oaths. They thus challenged civil authority on every level, since the Christianity of rulers, the use of weapons for defense and war, and the taking of oaths were serious matters in the sixteenth century. By refusing to participate Anabaptists were rejecting the legitimacy of the government. By insisting that civil authorities had no right to issue orders in religious matters, they were challenging a society in which religion and government were closely connected.[29]

So, the real reason behind the persecution of the Anabaptists may be that they were seen as a threat by both the church and civil society. "The identity of civic and religious community, as it had prevailed since the Emperor Constantine in the fourth century, was disrupted [by Anabaptist teaching]. The intense hostility of both ecclesiastical and the political establishments finds its explanation right here."[30] Whatever the motive from which it sprang, however, the persecution of the Anabaptists was fierce. The first to seal his witness with his blood was Felix Manz who was drowned in Zurich early in 1527. It is worthy of note that the official charge under which the martyrs were executed was usually sedition or perjury. Like that of Jesus the deaths of the Anabaptists were turned into a civil affair.

There are those who see the rise of Anabaptism as part of the Peasants' War, the last of a long series of south German uprisings against serfdom and lay and ecclesiastical abuse. Beginning in June 1524 rebellions swept through the area between the Rhine, Lech, and Danube Rivers. Petty burghers and restless knights banded together against spiritual leaders and territorial princes who had violated ancient local rights. They demanded, among other things, the elimination of the tithes to absentee clerics and the election of pastors. The rebels, however, could not match the well-provisioned soldiers and popular resistance collapsed but not before over 100,000 had been killed in what was tantamount to a civil war.

The insurgents had looked to Luther and his reforms for inspiration and support since they had suffered at the hands of abbots and bishops who used excommunication and other spiritual punishments to exploit those under their pastoral care. Luther's teachings condemning a greedy, tyrannical clergy seemed to give the peasants the right to revolt against the oppression. But Luther also condemned the rebels, insisting that the evangelical campaign against the papacy provided no warrant for civil insurrection. Without Luther's blessing, the Peasants' War lost its momentum, although it did weaken, if not abolish, serfdom and other feudal institutions in some areas.[31]

Although some consider Anabaptism a continuation of the Peasants' War, there are serious differences between the two movements. The peasants were motivated by a desire for social and economic change, not abstract theological principles. The peasants were demanding rights and powers, concepts rejected by the Anabaptists. The peasants did not reject all governments; the Anabaptists did. Indeed, had the peasants succeeded, the Anabaptists would have seen their government as unchristian. And most Anabaptists rejected outright the use of force. It remains true, however, that after the uprising failed, some of the peasants did turn to Anabaptism.[32]

ANABAPTIST THEOLOGY

Unlike the other reformers, Anabaptists did not see themselves "as a correction to, or lay monastic witness against, the compromises of an intact Christendom: they demanded a change of the whole pattern."[33]

The basic tenet of Anabaptism was that the church is a visible covenantal community; this is sometimes described as "kingdom theology." No distinctions were made between lay members and preachers, just as there was no division between sacred and secular. *Gemeinde*—community in the unity of the Spirit—was one of their guiding principles. Such a community, a real fellowship in the Lord, had to exist before the Lord's Supper could be celebrated.

The Anabaptists' concern for community led quite naturally to a disdain for private property. Everyone had an equal right to share in the goods of all, so the needy never went without help. Such a closeknit community of believers is essential for groups like the Anabaptists who hold a strong belief in a fundamental dualism which sees New Testament values as totally opposed to the values of the "world." Like other apocalyptic communities, the Anabaptists held that the kingdom was going to break in and the only way to be properly prepared was to separate from the world and all it stood for.[34]

Some of the other beliefs of these early Anabaptists can be gleaned from the oldest of the Anabaptist church orders, which originated with the first Anabaptist congregation in Bern, Switzerland.[35] There we find that there should be frequent assemblies; the first point of order was to be a mutual exhortation and there was to be conscientious instruction. In addition, there was emphasis on proper behavior: any break in regulations was to be punished. There is also a reminder that needy persons must not suffer, along with a directive calling for frequent celebration of the Lord's Supper, as well as the regularly practiced fellowship meal. Great moderation was enjoined, and believers were reminded that the Christian must always be prepared for the cross.

The accounts in *Martyrs' Mirror* make it clear that the Anabaptists were well versed in scripture. Obviously, they took the call to conscientious instruction seriously. The moving exhibit which led me to Elkhart on that Sunday afternoon reminded me of something else that had fired my imagination when I first met these gentle people: all of them, peasants or preachers, women or men, were prepared to answer whatever charges were thrown at them by their accusers. It is not just their boldness that is so striking but their competency: these were articulate martyrs. Mothers wrote to children, husbands bared their souls to wives, children looked on while their parents died, older ones holding smaller hands.

Anyone pondering this incredible chapter in the history of Christianity will readily acknowledge the Anabaptists' fidelity to another of their basic tenets: *Nachfolge*—obedience. God's word is revealed in scripture and, once that word has been heard and accepted, the only response is to obey. It is obedience more than discipleship that is the recurrent theme in many of the Anabaptist writings. Nor is this a blind obedience; the Anabaptists were aware of their inner freedom. They were also well aware of the weaknesses to which human nature is so prone but they trusted in God to give them the strength necessary to walk the path they had freely chosen. We have only to read the letters in *Martyrs' Mirror* to believe that they did find that strength.

WOMEN IN ANABAPTISM

"The army of God, which at this time prepared itself for the conflict and the sufferings of Jesus Christ, consisted not only of men, who are sometimes judged to be strongest, but also in women, for God's power is made strong in weakness."[36]

Sixteenth-century Anabaptist women achieved a prominence unparalleled in later generations, helping to carry forward the momentum of the radical reformation. Of the 900 martyrs in *Martyrs' Mirror*, nearly 300 were women.[37] In many ways, however, the role of women in Anabaptism was challenged by the general assumption in early modern Europe that prominent public positions belonged to the men.

Constrained by the pervasive societal tenor of their times, Anabaptists generally accepted a patriarchal structure although their extraordinary circumstances called women to a degree of equality uncommon in their day. Their acceptance of believers baptism also demanded that they acknowledge the basic equality of all their brothers and sisters as members of the spiritual body of Christ. Women, although forbidden to preach, teach, or baptize, helped to found and spread Anabaptist churches, donating their wealth and even their homes to the movement. The cohesiveness and warmth of Anabaptist congregational life also allowed for fuller participation by women. Historian C. H. Wedel points to this concept of fellowship and community as the most distinctive characteristic of Anabaptism,[38] while Daniel Liechty observes that Anabaptists formed "communities of real liberation in which the people involved set themselves to the task of restructuring their religious and social world together in ways which fostered the creative abilities of each person."[39]

In marriage, Anabaptists accepted the basic patriarchal family structure of their day. The husband was the head of the household—the wife was admonished to obey her husband. But to Anabaptists, marriage had a deeper meaning: the marital relationship of husband and wife was secondary to their mutual union with God. Anabaptist men often referred to their wives as "chosen," indicating not just a marriage free from parental arrangements but a conviction that God had brought the spouses together. Thus, both the physical and the spiritual aspects of marriage were important. The letters written by imprisoned Anabaptists are filled with deep faith and hope, but also with a great deal of tenderness and affection.[40]

In *Martyrs' Mirror*, marriage imagery is often used in connection with the martyrdom of women. Forced to forsake their earthly families, the martyrs will be welcomed by Christ, the heavenly bridegroom. So, while never rejecting the subordinate role of women that was part of the culture of their day, the Anabaptists willingly elevated them to the highest status a Christian could aspire to, that of martyr.[41]

The history of Anabaptism also contains many stories of women who, without any official approbation, assumed positions of leadership as apostles, prophetesses, and visionaries. Elizabeth of Leeuwarden, a leading figure in north Dutch Anabaptism who was martyred in Holland in 1549, was referred to as a *Leeraresse*, that is, someone who spoke or taught publicly.[42]

Both boys and girls were educated so they could read the scriptures. As a result, Anabaptist women brought up before priests and interrogators showed themselves well versed in scripture and resolute in their faith, equally at ease describing their personal commitment or defending points of Anabaptist doctrine. *Martyrs' Mirror* underscores the heroic example of the women of Anabaptism by preserving their stories, their letters and, in some cases, the record of their trials.

LETTERS OF HUSBANDS AND WIVES

Approximately one-third of the martyrs whose stories are told in *Martyrs' Mirror* are women. Van Braght depicts them as heroic and articulate, able to stand firm in the face of torture and death. But there are also numerous letters from imprisoned men to their wives. These letters offer moving testimony to the depth of both the love and the commitment of Anabaptist spouses. Many of the men admit that it is the certainty of their wives' support that allows them to face death without flinching.

Joris Wippe, imprisoned in the Hague in the Netherlands, entreats his wife: "O dear wife, pray the Lord for me as long as I am in this poor, weak flesh. I trust to remember you also in my prayers, and I most affectionately thank you in the Lord for sending me so kind an exhortation, which is food for the soul; I thank you also for the temporal things."[43]

Jelis Matthijss, before his death, wrote long treatises to his wife from Middelborgh, asking her to "assist me to thank and praise the merciful, dear Father, that I have safely come through the wilderness of this evil, wicked and perverse world." His last letter ends with the stark comment, "They have come for me." Like many of the martyrs, Matthijss for his part encourages his wife to remain steadfast, so that they may one day be reunited in glory.[44] Christian Langedul expresses this sentiment in the poignant opening of a letter to his wife, Maeyken: "My chosen and most affectionately beloved wife, and sister in the Lord because of the faith, as I hope by the grace of the Lord, and that this relationship will exist forever."[45]

Jan van Hasebroeck, imprisoned in Antwerp in Belgium, tells his wife, "O my beloved love, be pleased to know, that you were a medicine to my heart the last time I saw you at the lattice; for, as hart panteth after the water brooks, so did my heart long to see your face again."[46] Wives in these letters are addressed as "my dear," "my dear and much beloved," "my wife and sister in the Lord." Expressions of pain at imminent parting are common, as are requests for mutual forgiveness of any faults or shortcomings. Another martyr of Antwerp, Joost Verkindert, writes:

Hence, my beloved, help me heartily to entreat the Lord, that He will preserve me through His great goodness and longsuffering as the apple of His eye, that I may not be seduced through philosophy or carnal liberty, nor depart from my God, of which I have a great terror; but that He will comfort

and strengthen me in my good purpose, to the praise of His holy name, and
to the salvation of my soul.[47]

Martyrs' Mirror also preserves letters written by imprisoned Anabaptist wives to their husbands. Men are addressed as "my dear
husband," and "my beloved husband in the Lord." Like the men's
letters, these are filled with love, sorrow at separation, and mutual
encouragement. The women are apparently as versed as the men in
scripture; the letters abound with biblical quotations and citations.
Lijsken, writing to Jerome in Antwerp, is typical:

My beloved husband in the Lord, know that at first the time seemed very
long to me, because I was not used to imprisonment, and heard nothing but
temptations to depart from the Lord. . . . But it is sufficient for us, that we
have believed. . . . Be of good cheer therefore, my most beloved in the Lord,
and rejoice in Him as before, praising and thanking him for having chosen
us to be imprisoned so long for His name.[48]

Adriaenken Jans wrote to her husband shortly before her death
in Dortrecht. She assures him she is well, and, while she can do
nothing to change her fate, she intends to leave him "a few lines in
remembrance of me, on account of the great love which we have had
to each other, and which I hope will abide forever." She wants to
comfort her husband and bids him look forward to a glorious future.
"Thus, my cordially beloved husband and dearest brother in the
Lord, I your specially, cordially beloved wife, Adriaenken Jans, your
dearest sister in the Lord, who have married each other before the
Lord and His church, I will herewith bid your love adieu, and await
you there with your and our dearest Bridegroom, Christ Jesus."[49]

Mothers in prison wrote poignant letters to their children.
Maeyken Wens wrote to her oldest son, Adriaen, from her prison in
Antwerp:

My dear child Adriaen, my son, I leave you this for a testament, because you
are the oldest, to exhort you that you should begin to fear our dear Lord, for
you are getting old enough to perceive what is good or evil. . . . My son, from
your youth follow that which is good and depart from evil. . . . This I,
Maeyken Wens, your mother, have written while I was in prison for the word
of the Lord; the good Father grant you his grace, my son Adriaen.[50]

In Rotterdam in the Netherlands, Maeyken van Deventer wrote to
her children: "My children in the flesh, I must leave you young; may
the Most High permit us to meet in the world to come, . . . thank the
Most High, that you had a mother who was found worthy to shed her
blood for the name of the Lord, and who, through his grace and
mercy, may be counted as a witness or martyr." She then writes a

lengthy instruction for the children, which she urges them to keep as her testament.[51]

Fifteen-year-old Adriaen "could not stay away from the place of execution on the day on which his dear mother was offered up." With his little brother, he took up a position near the stakes, but fainted. When it was all over, he "hunted in the ashes, in which he found the screw with which her tongue had been screwed fast, which he kept in remembrance of her." Van Braght adds that in 1659, several of Maeyken's grandchildren were still alive.[52]

WOMEN MARTYRS

Although occasionally treated less severely than their male counterparts, Anabaptist women imprisoned for their belief were subject to cruel tortures and death by fire or drowning. In the sixteenth century torture was fairly standard, used to extract information or, as in the case of the Anabaptists, a confession.

The physical pain of the torture itself was compounded for the women by the custom of undressing victims as part of the procedure. Klassen observes that what "strikes the modern reader is that the women expressed greater distress over their state of undress than they did over the torture."[53]

The letters in *Martyrs' Mirror* also indicate that, like most prisoners in medieval and early modern times, the Anabaptists awaiting execution had to supply their own fuel, food and drink, and bedding.[54] The women often preferred more spiritual support. When Aeltgen Baten's husband sent her money and blankets, she refused them. Her young companion, Maeyken Wouters, wrote to her parents asking them not to attempt to ransom her but to send her letters of comfort, the only thing she needed.[55]

Perhaps to underscore the important place these women occupy in the history of Anabaptism, the first martyr book, *Het Offer des Heeren* (1562 edition) placed the story of Anneken Jans right after that of Michael Sattler, who is often considered the ultimate symbol of Anabaptist fidelity. A former monk, Sattler, by now married to Margaretha, a beguine, arrived in Zurich and became embroiled in the controversies there. Apparently well educated, Sattler wrote extensively, delineating Anabaptist theology and explicating Anabaptist doctrine.

When the movement was in danger of breaking up after the death or exile of the early leaders, it was Sattler who stepped in and helped them regroup. His is generally considered the hand behind the Schleitheim Confession, the 1527 document that marked the turning point in Anabaptism between a largely informal sect and a mature movement "taking responsibility for its order and its faith."[56] Because of his importance to the movement Sattler was subjected to

Anabaptist Anneken Jans Drowned at Rotterdam, 1539. Courtesy of Lancaster Mennonite Historical Society, 2215 Millstream Road, Lancaster, PA 17602-1499.

Anabaptists Maria and Ursula van Beckum Burned at Deventer, 1544. Courtesy of Lancaster Mennonite Historical Society, 2215 Millstream Road, Lancaster, PA 17602-1499.

Two Young Anabaptist Ladies Executed in the Bishopric of Bamberg, 1550. Courtesy of Lancaster Mennonite Historical Society, 2215 Millstream Road, Lancaster, PA 17602-1499.

a mockery of a trial and had to undergo unspeakable tortures before finally being burned at the stake in Rotterdam in May of 1527. Eight days later his wife was drowned in the Neckar. Word of Sattler's execution spread throughout Germany, Austria, and Switzerland. In death, he became an undying witness to the Anabaptist movement.[57]

Anneken Jans, who is identified in *Martyrs' Mirror* as Anna of Rotterdam, wrote a testimony to her son, Isaiah, shortly before her death in 1539. She tells him she is going "the way of the prophets, apostles and martyrs, [to] drink of the cup of which they have all drank," and goes on to describe the biblical lineage of martyrs in some detail. She then exhorts her son to follow the right path, confident in the loving care of the Lord.[58]

Women were resolute and prepared to answer their interrogators. The account of Maria van Beckum and her sister-in-law, Ursula, illustrates this. After several attempts to change their views failed, a "commissary came from the court of Burgundy, who greatly extolled the mass and all the institutions of the pope; but he could not prevail against the Scriptures which they adduced." Brought into open court, Maria and Ursula were sentenced to death but continued to witness even on their way to the stake, proclaiming, "Weep not on account of what is inflicted on us. We do not suffer as witches or other criminals, but because we adhere to Christ, and will not be separated from God; hence be converted, and it shall be well with you forever."[59]

Martyrs' Mirror preserves verbatim an interrogation of Elizabeth Dirks, arrested in Holland in January of 1549. Elizabeth is described as a "teacheress" and the wife of Menno Simons. Simons, a former Catholic priest, became such an influential leader in Dutch Anabaptism that the group later became known as Mennonites.[60] There is no evidence that he and Elizabeth were married; she herself tells the interrogator that she has no husband. She was, however, well-versed in scripture and apparently able to read Latin. Despite harsh interrogation and then physical torture, Elizabeth refused to identify other Anabaptists and was finally drowned. More than 400 years after her death, her composure in the most frightening circumstances is still amazing.

Lords: We shall make you so afraid, that you will tell us.

Elizabeth: I hope through the grace of God, that He will keep my tongue, so that I shall not become a traitoress, and deliver my brother unto death.

Lords: What persons were present when you were baptized?

Elizabeth: Christ said: Ask them that were present, or who heard it. John 18:21. . . .

Lords: What are your views concerning infant baptism, seeing you have been rebaptized?

Elizabeth: No, my lords, I have not been rebaptized. I have been baptized once upon my faith; for it is written that baptism belongs to believers.

Having failed in their attempts to break her, the council offered Elizabeth one last chance.

Lords: Will you revoke all that you have previously confessed here?

Elizabeth: No, my lords, but I will seal it with my death.[61]

One of the more poignant woodcuts in *Martyrs' Mirror* shows two young girls being led to execution. Although their names are not recorded, their steadfastness in enduring torture and accepting death belied their youth. The woodcut shows the crowd placing crowns of straw on the girls' heads. When this was done, one said to the other, "Since the Lord Christ wore a crown of thorns for us, why should we not wear these crowns of straw in honor of Him? The faithful God shall for this place a beautiful golden crown wreath upon our heads."[62]

Jerome Segers and his wife, Lijsken Dircks, were both imprisoned in Antwerp. *Martyrs' Mirror* preserves a remarkable exchange of letters between the two. Jerome was executed but Lijsken remained in prison, perhaps because she was pregnant. It had become customary to allow pregnant women to deliver before facing death; the babies were then given to orthodox families or sometimes to convents. Despite repeated attempts to get her to recant, Lijsken remained faithful even preaching and singing hymns from the window of her cell. To prevent her death from becoming the occasion of a supportive rally, her captors "perpetrated their murderous work between three and four o'clock [in the morning]. They took the lamb to the Scheldt, thrust her into a bag, and drowned her, before the people arrived, so that but few witnessed it." The strategy backfired, however, since the people, on learning what had happened, were outraged at the "thieves and murderers" who had acted in such a cruel manner.[63]

The account of the death of Felistis Jan is informative, since it contains a summary of the charges against her taken from the original criminal records of Amsterdam.

1. That she had resorted to the assembly of the sect of the Anabaptists.
2. That she had separated from the obedience and faith of the (so-called) holy (that is, Roman) church.
3. That she held pernicious views with regard to the sacrament of the altar.

4. That she had harbored in her house such persons as she knew to belong to said sect (that is, the sect of the so-called Anabaptists).

5. That she had seduced several persons from the obedience of the (Roman) church, to her belief.

6. That she herself obstinately adhered to the aforementioned (so-called) errors, refusing to abandon them.

7. That all this was contrary to the ordinances of the holy church, and the decrees of his Imperial Majesty.

Felistis was condemned, first to torture, then to death by fire. She is described as virtuous and honorable and once refused to perform an errand that would take her outside her cell, lest the temptation to escape be too powerful to resist. Before being led to the stake, Felistis put on clean clothes and a white apron, "as though by her outward garments she meant to indicate how purely and uprightly a Christian virgin ought to be adorned inwardly, in order to be acceptable before her beloved heavenly bridegroom, Christ Jesus."[64]

ANABAPTIST WOMEN AND CHOICE

Felistis' refusal to put herself into circumstances that would tempt her to escape is worthy of note. Jenifer Umble has examined this aspect of choice among the women of *Martyrs' Mirror.* Taking her cue from an earlier article by Sherrin Wyntjes,[65] Umble examines the nature of the choices made by the Anabaptist women,[66] finding numerous examples of both active and passive choices. The women "actively" chose to join the sect and to remain steadfast even in the face of imprisonment, torture, and death. They "passively" accepted persecution as the natural consequence of being numbered among God's elect.

Umble draws attention to the unique essence of Anabaptism that "emphasized more dramatically than did other forms of Protestantism the commitment between the individual and God."[67] Anabaptist customs put the members at odds with their neighbors and also made them easy to identify.

While some women did choose to avoid capture, *Martyrs' Mirror* contains a number of women who chose to face arrest when they could have escaped. Umble cites the case of Christian Haring who was released from prison to have a baby. When the time came she was willingly rearrested.[68] Even when local authorities gave sufficient warning to the Anabaptists about imminent arrests, many chose to remain.

Although the accounts do not speculate on the motivation behind these choices, van Braght believes that the women accepted their fate out of deep faith and commitment. Umble adds, once the threat of arrest had become reality Anabaptists were free to proclaim their faith publicly. "A woman might hesitate to proclaim her beliefs publicly in the face of persecution. Yet the certainty of martyrdom following arrest freed her to declare her faith."[69]

Nor did the need to choose end with arrest. *Martyrs' Mirror* records several interrogations during which women could have chosen to renounce their beliefs, but opted instead to defend Anabaptist doctrine. Besides rigorous questioning, the women were subjected to other strategies designed to force them to recant, such as torture, the offer of money, and even marriage proposals. "The bailiff promised freedom and one year's living expenses to Maria of Monjou, provided she would attend the Catholic church. Her captors first threatened Nelleken Jaspers, a young girl of eighteen, with horrible death, then enticed her with promises of marriage, should she recant. . . . A chaplain endeavored to overcome Maeyken Wouters with a 'can of wine.'"[70]

The choices made by these women reflect what has come to be called the Anabaptist "theology of suffering" that viewed persecution as a natural consequence of being numbered among the elect, and therefore a mark of true discipleship.[71] That is why so many of the letters and testimonies reflect the women's gratitude that they have been found worthy to suffer. In a sense, then, all their choices were active ones. Umble concludes: "Whether they perceived adherence to Anabaptism to be the will of God or a conscious individual decision, the choices of these women may be described as *active* in the sense that their decisions reveal a strength of purpose, a determination, a conscious decision to persist in their beliefs."[72]

ANABAPTIST HYMNODY

The Anabaptist experience of persecution and martyrdom was reflected in their hymns, many of which were written by women. Hymns are theology set to music, and Anabaptists apparently took every opportunity to sing out their witness. "Anabaptists sang in prison; they sang on their way to the stake; they sang to express their joy and their trust."[73] Van Braght tells of a woman from Bruges who sang Psalm 27 as her death sentence was being pronounced. He goes on to say that "the people firmly believed that if they had not gagged her when they brought her to the place of execution, she would have departed this life singing and praising God."[74]

Kreider describes Anabaptist hymn writing as "an act of resistance, in which spirituality and social nonconformity are thoroughly integrated." He cites as an example a hymn based on Isaiah 59:14, "Justice is turned back, and righteousness stands afar off; for truth has fallen in the public squares and uprightness cannot enter."[75]

Van Braght indicates in several cases that a martyr's story or last words have been set down as a hymn but only a few are actually included in *Martyrs' Mirror.* One celebrates the witness and courageous death of Adriaenken Jans, the young woman of Molenaersgraef who had written so movingly to her husband and who, along with Jan Wouters, was executed in Dortrecht in 1572:

> Jan Wouterss clearly spake:
> This is the day of salvation.
> Be silent, said the underbailiff.
> Why should I, he said, forbear to speak?
> My words are neither bad nor bold.
> Adriaenken too looked forward,
> To please her Bridegroom.
> She rests now in the Lord,
> And has passed the fire's pain. . . .
> These two lambs have now passed through,
> Away tempest!
> What were now all their sufferings?
> They obtained the martyr's crown,
> Which now they hold as their reward.[76]

These hymns were later collected in the *Ausbund,* the first Mennonite hymnbook. Originally published in German in 1564 the *Ausbund* is still used by the descendants of the Anabaptistis, such as the Old Order Amish, making it the oldest Protestant hymnal still in use. The nucleus of the *Ausbund* was some 50 hymns collected by a group of Swiss Brethren imprisoned in Bavaria in 1535. The martyrs' hymns in the *Ausbund* describe the suffering and piety of the early Anabaptists, as well as the date and manner of their death.[77]

CONCLUSION

"Anabaptism was essentially a movement which insisted upon an earnest and uncompromising endeavor to live a life of true discipleship of Christ, that is to give expression in fellowship and love to the deepest Christian faith, with full readiness to suffer in conflict with the evil world order."[78] The central tenet of Anabaptist faith is that God does, indeed, tent among us and it is imperative that each generation pass the stories along to the one that succeeds it. So

Maeyken van Deventer's instruction to her children is just as powerful today as it was when she first wrote it. Anneken Jans speaks across the centuries, not just to her own son, but to all Christians in every age.

Yet, the question remains: so what? What do these martyrs, these courageous, radical women of another time and place, far removed from our own, have to do with us? What can we, with our modern, high-tech society, hope to gain from contemplating the lives and deaths of a band of valiant women and men who chose to die rather than conform to what seemed to them a watered-down Christianity? It would appear there is much to gain by looking into this mirror, by gazing deeply into the eyes that are reflected back into our own.

Christianity in late-twentieth-century America has become a matter of convenience. The same affluence which watered down the Christian message in the centuries after Constantine is watering down American Christianity today. We need to stand before the *Martyrs' Mirror* and gaze into the faces we see there, faces from long ago, faces of ordinary men and women, faces that remind us that, whatever it is meant to be, Christianity was never meant to be convenient.

Also we need to look around our world and see that the age of martyrs has not passed. Not only are people still dying for their beliefs but governments are still hiding behind labels like "subversive" to justify their deaths. *Martyrs' Mirror* serves as an example, a reminder that the stories, especially the women's stories, need to be told. As a Roman Catholic I find it ironic that it took the commercial film industry to tell the story of Jean Donovan, a young laywoman who died in El Salvador along with three Catholic sisters in 1980.[79] Where are the books for young readers, the updated collections of the lives of the saints that were so popular when I was growing up in the 1950s and 1960s? We are missing a wonderful opportunity to fire the minds and hearts of our young people with stories of contemporary Christians who are living out what we all claim to believe. Our own commitment, too, would be given a boost by hearing that a Christian really can make a difference.

We may not all be called to shed our blood for Christ but we are all called to follow his example. We are the latest inheritors of a tradition that calls us to make the Kingdom of God present in the world here and now. We are called to be countercultural.

The women of *Martyrs' Mirror* assure us that such a stance is possible; indeed they literally sing out from the scaffolds, proclaiming their trust in God and urging us to trust no less. Let us listen to van Braght in his preface to *Martyrs' Mirror*: "Read it again and again. . . . if you do this, it will not be unfruitful to you. But, before all things, fix your eyes upon the martyrs themselves, note the stead-fastness of their faith, and follow their example."[80] This is a noble endeavor; the time to begin is now.

NOTES

1. John Klassen, "Women and the Family among Dutch Anabaptist Martyrs," *Mennonite Quarterly Review* (hereafter *MQR*) 60 (1986), p. 558. Although Anabaptism was not confined to any one geographic location, it began in Switzerland and many of the martyrs introduced in this chapter met their fate in Switzerland, Belgium, and the Netherlands.

2. Tielman J. van Braght, *The Bloody Theatre or Martyrs' Mirror of the Defenseless Christians.* Translated from the edition of 1660 by J. F. Sohm (Scottdale, PA: Herald Press, 1950), hereafter *MM*.

3. The last Anabaptist martyr in the northern Netherlands died in 1574; the last in the south died in 1597.

4. William R. Estep, *The Anabaptist Story: An Introduction to Sixteenth-Century Anabaptism* 3rd Edition (Grand Rapids, MI: William B. Eerdmans Publishing Company, 1996), pp. 10–11.

5. The so-called "Great Schism" of 1378–1417 was a period of crisis in the Western church, during which first two and then three rivals claimed papal authority. In 1409 the Council of Pisa deposed Popes Benedict XIII and Gregory XII, and elected Alexander V as pontiff. But, since neither Benedict nor Gregory accepted the council's decision, the church found itself with three "popes." Finally, at the Council of Constance (1414–1418), Pope John XXII (Alexander's successor) was deposed and Martin V was elected as the one pope of the Roman church, while Gregory resigned and Benedict fled.

6. The inquisition will be discussed more fully in the next chapter.

7. Roland H. Bainton, *The Reformation of the Sixteenth Century* (Boston: Beacon Press, 1952), p. 15.

8. Cornelius J. Dyck, ed., *An Introduction to Mennonite History: A Popular History of the Anabaptists and the Mennonites* (Scottdale, PA: Herald Press, 1981), p. 27.

9. Dyke, *Introduction*, pp. 28–29.

10. Carter Lindberg, *The European Reformations* (Cambridge, MA: Blackwell Publishers Inc., 1996), pp. 45–46.

11. Dyck, *Introduction*, p. 28.

12. The teaching on indulgences is intimately connected to a concept of salvation which includes a time of cleansing for the soul between death and ultimate union with God in heaven; this is the state commonly known as "purgatory." Indulgences are also an outgrowth of the development, during the early Middle Ages, of the system of "tariff penance," according to which difficult penances were commuted to a specified number of prayers or a specified amount of almsgiving.

13. The granting of indulgences was outlined in three stages. Stage one was the crusaders themselves, whose fighting was deemed the equivalent of staying home and performing mandatory penances. The second stage

concerned those who contributed directly to the wars. The third stage covered, by extension, those who raised money for the construction of hospitals, bridges, and cathedrals. The theory behind indulgences was that Christ and the saints had stored up "superfluous" merits, that is, more than they needed for their personal salvation. These "credits" were stored in the church's "treasury" and could be transferred by the pope to those who needed them. See Bainton, *Reformation*, pp. 13–14.

14. Dyck, *Introduction*, p. 24.

15. A lay preacher of the late twelfth century, Valdes of Lyons, commonly referred to as Peter Waldo, gave away his wealth to become an itinerant preacher. He and his followers, the Poor Men of Lyons, ignored Alexander III's request that they not preach in public. The Waldensians were declared heretics in 1184 and suffered intermittent persecution. They survive today, especially in northwestern Italy.

16. The Index was a list of books Catholics were forbidden to read or even to own, under penalty of excommunication. Established by Pope Paul IV in 1557, the Index was used to ban works thought to contain material contrary to faith and/or morals. Pope Paul VI abolished the Index in 1966 as inconsistent with Vatican II's espousal of freedom of inquiry.

17. W. David Myers, "Erasmus, Desiderius," and (no author cited), "Index of Forbidden Books," in Richard P. McBrien et al., eds., *The Harpercollins Encyclopedia of Catholicism* (San Francisco: Harper San Francisco, 1995), pp. 474–475 and p. 661.

18. All of this information is available in a variety of sources, but I am also indebted to Prof. James F. White, for his lectures in the Reformation Liturgies seminar at Notre Dame.

19. John C. Wenger, *Even Unto Death: The Heroic Witness of the Sixteenth-Century Anabaptists* (Richmond, VA: John Knox Press, 1961), pp. 15, 17–18.

20. Bainton, *Reformation*, p. 95.

21. Dyck, *Introduction*, pp. 44–45.

22. "Anabaptist" comes from a Latin derivative of the Greek *anababtismos*, rebaptism. The German term is *wiedertäufer*. The group themselves repudiated this, both because infant baptism was not their core issue and because, since they considered infant baptism nonexistent, theirs was not a second baptism. They preferred simply *Brüder*, the Brethren. "Baptism became important only because it was the most obvious dividing line between two patterns of church organization." See Franklin H. Littell, *The Anabaptist View of the Church* Second Edition (Boston: Beacon Hill, 1958), p. xv.

23. Bainton, *Reformation*, p. 97.

24. Josef von Beck, ed., *Die Geschichts-Bücher der Wiedertäufer in Oesterreich-Ungarn* (Vienna: Carl Gerold's Sohn, 1883), pp. 12, 13, cited in Littell, *Anabaptist View*, p. 2.

25. Bainton, *Reformation*, pp. 98–99. Donatism, which arose in North Africa during the third and fourth centuries, was an attempt to return to the integrity, holiness, and self-sacrifice of the pre-Constantinian church. One of its teachings was that sacraments administered by sinful priests

were invalid, so many people joining the groups received a new baptism. Augustine, in the fifth century, developed his doctrines concerning the true nature of the church and its sacraments in his campaign against the Donatists. At the same time, he justified repression by the church of any movements or individuals deemed heretical. See W.H.C. Frend, "Donatism," in Everett Ferguson, ed., *Encyclopedia of Early Christianity* (New York: Garland Publishing, Inc., 1990), pp. 274–277. Bainton sees significant parallels between the Donatist and Anabaptist movements.

26. Hans-Jürgen Goertz, *The Anabaptists* Second Edition (New York: Routledge, 1988), p. 119.

27. Littell, *Anabaptist View*, pp. 12–15.

28. Von Beck, *Geschichtsbücher*, cited in E. Belfort Bax, *Rise and Fall of the Anabaptists* (reprint) (New York: Augustus M. Kelley, Publishers, 1970 [1903]), p. 4.

29. Claus-Peter Clasen, *Anabaptism: A Social History, 1525–1618* (Ithaca: Cornell University Press, 1972), pp. 172–175, 180–181.

30. Daniel Liechty, trans. and ed., *Early Anabaptist Spirituality: Selected Writings* (New York: Paulist Press, 1994), pp. xvi–xvii.

31. See George Huntston Williams, *The Radical Reformation* (Philadelphia: The Westminster Press, 1962), pp. 59–60.

32. Clasen, *Anabaptism*, pp. 153–155.

33. Littell, *Anabaptist View*, p. 4.

34. Robert Friedmann, *The Theology of Anabaptists* (Scottdale, PA: Herald Press, 1973), pp. 40–41.

35. This information is readily available from many sources. I am using R. Friedmann, *The Theology of Anabaptism* (Scottdale, PA: Herald Press, 1973) pp. 126–127.

36. Van Braght, *MM*, p. 1120.

37. Keith L. Sprunger, "God's Powerful Army of the Weak: Anabaptist Women of the Radical Reformation," in R. L. Greaves, ed., *Triumph over Silence: Women in Protestant History* (Westport: Greenwood Press, 1985), pp. 46–47.

38. The Anabaptist *Gemeindekirche* (church of fellowship) differed in this respect from the authoritarian *Priesterkirche* (church of priests) of the Catholics and the *Staatskirche* (church of the state) of the other reformers. See Coendrius H. Wedel, *Abriss der Geschicte der Mennoniten* (Newton, KS: Schulverlag von Bethel-College, 1900–1904), Vol. 2, pp. 147–159; Vol. 4, pp. 206–208.

39. Leichty, *Early Anabaptist*, p. 13.

40. Klassen, "Women and the Family," pp. 554–561; Sprunger, "God's Powerful Army," pp. 57–58.

41. Lois Barrett, "The Role and Influence of Anabaptist Women in the Martyr Story," *Brethren Life and Thought* 37 (Spring 1992), p. 88.

42. Sprunger, "God's Powerful Army," p. 53.

43. *MM*, p. 586.

44. *MM*, p. 680.

45. *MM*, p. 704.

46. *MM*, p. 770.

47. *MM*, p. 860.

48. *MM*, p. 515.

49. *MM*, pp. 926–927.

50. *MM*, pp. 981–982.

51. *MM*, p. 980.

52. *MM*, pp. 977–979.

53. Klassen, "Women and the Family," p. 553.

54. See J. Bellamy, *Crime and Public Order in England in the Later Middle Ages* (London: Routledge and Kegan Paul, 1973).

55. *MM*, pp. 1091–1092.

56. John H. Yoder, *The Legacy of Michael Sattler* (Scottdale, PA: Herald Press, 1973), p. 29.

57. Estep, *Anabaptist Story*, pp. 57–73.

58. *MM*, p. 453. There has been considerable scholarly debate over the historical accuracy of the accounts of Anna's life and martyrdom. The question is not whether the events occurred, but whether Anna was a member of the so-called Jorist faction of Anabaptism, a faction disowned by Menno Simons and his followers. See Werner O. Packull, "Anna Jansz of Rotterdam, a Historical Investigation of an Early Anabaptist Martyr," *Archiv für Reformationsgeschichte* 78 (1987): pp. 147–173.

59. *MM*, p. 467.

60. See Estep, *Anabaptist Story*, pp. 160–174.

61. *MM*, pp. 481–483.

62. *MM*, p. 500.

63. *MM*, pp. 504–522.

64. *MM*, p. 539.

65. Sherrin Marshall Wyntjes, "Women and Religious Choices in the Sixteenth Century Netherlands," *Archiv für Reformationsgeschichte* 75 (1984), pp. 276–289.

66. Jenifer Hiett Umble, "Women and Choice: An Examination of the *Martyrs' Mirror*," *MQR* 64 (April 1990), pp. 135–145.

67. Umble, "Women," p. 136.

68. *MM*, p. 441.

69. Umble, "Women," p. 140.

70. Umble, "Women," p. 142; *MM*, pp. 525, 762, 1091.

71. See A. Orly Swartzentruber, "The Piety and Theology of the Anabaptist Martyrs in van Braght's *Martyrs' Mirror*," *MQR* 28 (1954), pp. 129–131; Ethelbert Stauffer, "The Anabaptist Theology of Martyrdom," *MQR* 19 (1945), pp. 179–214; and Walter Klassen, ed., *Anabaptism Revisited* (Scottdale, PA: Herald Press, 1992), esp. pp. 85–97.

72. Umble, "Women," p. 145.

73. Alan Kreider, "The Relevance of *Martyrs' Mirror* to our Time," *Mennonite Life* (September 1990), p. 11.

74. *MM*, p. 738.

75. Kreider, "Revelance," p. 11.

76. *MM*, pp. 897–901.

77. Ernest A. Payne, "The Anabaptists," in G. R. Elton, ed., *The New Cambridge Modern History: The Reformation 1520–1559* Volume 2 (Cam-

bridge: Cambridge University Press, 1962), p. 132; Gerald C. Studer, "A History of the *Martyrs' Mirror*," *MQR* 22 (1948), p. 167; James F. White, *Protestant Worship: Traditions in Transition* (Louisville, KY: Westminster John Knox Press, 1989), p. 86.

78. Leonard Gross, "Recasting the Anabaptist Vision: The Longer View," *MQR* 60 (July 1986), p. 361.

79. The reference is to the television movie "Choices of the Heart," in which Melissa Gilbert portrayed Jean Donovan.

80. *MM*, p. 8.

3

Victims of the Witch Craze: Scapegoats in a Time of Turmoil

Witch-hunts were neither small in scope nor implemented by a few aberrant individuals; the persecution of witches was the official policy of both the Catholic and Protestant Churches. The Church invented the crime of witch-craft, established the process by which to prosecute it, and then insisted that witches be prosecuted. . . . Under the pretext of heresy and then witchcraft, anyone could be disposed of who questioned authority or the Christian view of the world. Witch-hunting secured the conversion of Europe to orthodox Christianity. Through the terror of the witch-hunts, reformational Christians convinced common people to believe that a singular male God reigned from above, that he was separate from earth, that magic was evil, that there was a powerful devil, and that women were most likely to be his agents.[1]

PROLOGUE

Each year, thousands of visitors pour into Trier in the picturesque Moselle Valley in southwestern Germany. Considered the oldest city in Germany, Trier was founded as Augusta Treverorum in 15 BCE, and, as Roma Secunda, served as a provincial capital of the western Roman Empire in the third century of the Christian era. Tourists delight in the ancient Roman gate, the baths, the museums, and the Hauptmarkt, the main square with its 1,000-year-old market cross.

What most of these visitors don't realize is that, just 300 years ago, other groups flocked to this square, and hundreds like it in small towns and cities throughout western Europe, not to see the sights but to watch women burn. Under the patronage of Johann von Schöneburg, who began his reign in Trier in 1581, "the campaign of Trier was of an importance quite unique in the history of witchcraft. In twenty-two villages 368 witches were burnt between 1587 and 1593, and two villages, in 1585, were left with only one female inhabitant apiece."[2] The cross in the square at Trier is a reminder, for those who know the story, that the Christianization of Europe cost lives.[3]

HISTORICAL BACKGROUND

"Historical European witchcraft is quite simply a fiction, in the sense that there is no evidence that witches existed, still less that they celebrated black masses or worshipped strange gods."[4]

The fourteenth century in western Europe had been marked by political and cultural dislocations. Terrible economic and social crises resulted from wars and famines, and there was a long series of plagues, most famously the Black Death of 1347–1349.[5] A growing population was suddenly reduced while economic and social institutions like feudalism were being restructured. Farms, villages, and manors were deserted and the growing power of the emerging merchant and industrial classes was leading to a new sense of alienation and a loss of faith in the church that appeared powerless to protect the masses from all these upheavals.[6] The times called for a scapegoat; one answer was the increasing hostility toward women that ultimately expressed itself in the period of the witch-hunts.

In medieval theology the feminine symbolized the physical, lustful, material, appetitive part of human nature, while the masculine symbolized the spiritual, rational, and mental part. This, combined with the negative view of marriage and sexuality characteristic of the period, resulted in the justified oppression of women and provided the basis for "the witch-hunting theology that labeled elderly women as fleshly and irrational, even diabolical."[7]

The *Canon Episcopi* of 906 declared a belief in witchcraft heretical. The canon, which remained in effect from the tenth through the thirteenth century, directed bishops to strive to uproot all kinds of sorcery and magic since these were the means the devil used to deceive people into thinking witchcraft was real and thus abandoning the true God of Christianity. In other words, witchcraft itself was a delusion but one that was capable of undermining the church.[8]

By the twelfth century, however, frightening images of devils and witches on broomsticks began to appear. The church was now portraying witches in terms usually applied to heretics: "a small clandestine society engaged in antihuman practices, including infanticide, incest, cannibalism, bestiality and orgiastic sex."[9] Scholasticism, the medieval theology developed in the universities, was one force that changed the attitude toward witches. According to the Scholastics, the deeds of the witches were absolutely real. In his *Summa Theologica*, Thomas Aquinas makes this quite clear and it is, according to Julio Baroja, the work of Aquinas that "goes far to explain the increased violence of persecution and the categorical return to the doctrine laid down in Exodus 22:18: 'Thou shalt not suffer a witch to live.'"[10]

Stuart Clark notes that "in the sixteenth and seventeenth centuries a predisposition to see things in terms of binary opposition was a distinctive aspect of a prevailing mentality." In this period marked by a "preoccupation with the extreme poles of the religious and moral universe," witchcraft beliefs represented the orthodox world reversed or inverted to such an extent that every facet of demonism was read as an actual or symbolic inversion of traditional life.[11] Indeed, sanctity and witchcraft were sometimes regarded as mirror images of each other.[12]

While the relationship between the holy and unholy could be studied in virtually any historical context, it was in late medieval Europe that it became a particularly important issue, partly because society was increasingly complex: rising lay literacy gave wider access to spiritual literature and spiritual exercises, and the proliferation of religious orders, societies, and movements brought with it an unwieldy assortment of folk whose multiform pious activities were met with equally manifold distrust. Perhaps never before in the history of Christianity. . . . were there so many people distrustful of each other's pieties. What could be more natural in such a culture than suspicions, first whispered and then shouted aloud, that the pretense of sanctity was a mask for the worst form of impiety?[13]

Where prior to the fifteenth century people had distinguished between "white witchcraft," or healing, and "black witchcraft," or evil, in the sixteenth and seventeenth centuries a third category emerged, "evolved by churchmen and lawyers from Christian theology, canon law and certain philosophical ideas. . . . The witch became a witch by virtue of a personal arrangement with the Devil who appeared to his potential recruit in some physical form."[14]

As the Inquisition was developed to rid the true church of heretics, so now its powers were extended to deal with the even greater danger of women in league with the devil. Witches were perceived to be the mirror image of true mystics: as true mystics experienced God, so these women experienced communion with the devil; . . . The engagement of ecclesiastical authority with who should count as a mystic, and its gendered nature, could hardly be clearer.[15]

"The papacy and the Inquisition had successfully transformed the witch from a phenomenon whose existence the Church had previously rigorously denied into a phenomenon that was deemed very real, very frightening, the antithesis of Christiantiy, and absolutely deserving of persecution."[16]

THE INQUISITION

"While moral justice was impossible, given the presupposition of the Church that it had the right, even the duty, to persecute those who differed in their religious beliefs, legal justice in sixteenth-century terms *was* indeed dispensed by the Roman Inquisition."[17]

By the early Middle Ages heresy had been "clearly defined as organized groups of people propagating ideas that represented more than simple opposition to the Church, and which threatened the basis of medieval society."[18] The church was becoming increasingly centralized and powerful, a reality that "reached its zenith during the pontificate of Innocent III (1198–1216), the first and most important of the great lawyer-popes who dominated the thirteenth century."[19] "Heresy is an invention of the Middle Ages. From about the eleventh century, churchmen increasingly worried about heresy, and in 1179 the Third Lateran Council issued a strong decree against the various forms which it believed it could discern. From that point forward, the inquisitors were kept busy hunting heretics and seeking to purge the church of them."[20]

Prior to Pope Innocent III there had already been a gradual shift from a reluctant tolerance of heresy to persecution of the offenders. In 1184 the first sign of an official policy appeared in the form of a bull, *Ad abolendam*, issued by Pope Lucius III. The bull ordered bishops to "make inquisition" for heresy, but local bishops proved ineffective. It was left to Innocent to conceive of a coordinated policy.

When Innocent called the Lateran Council in 1215 he had two main objectives: the Holy Land crusades and the suppression of heresy. Canon 3 specified harsh measures against heretics and warned "lax" bishops that they would be removed from their posts. The Inquisition itself dates to the early pontificate of Pope Gregory IX, becoming a reality sometime between 1227 and 1233. In 1231 the constitution *Excommunicamus* contained detailed legislation for the punishment of heretics. Gregory entrusted this work to the Mendicant Orders founded by Dominic and Francis. "The enthusiasm with which some of them took to this new task, . . . represents one of the most curious episodes in the history of the church."[21]

Pope Innocent IV, in the bull *Ad Extirpanda*, declared civil power subservient to the Inquisition, insisting that the uprooting of heresy was the chief duty of the state and introducing torture into inquisitorial procedure. The bull also condoned burning at the stake for relapsed heretics. In 1298 the system of repression instituted by Innocent III and honed by popes Alexander IV, Urban IV, and Clement IV, was codified by Pope Boniface VIII in his *Liber Sextus*.[22] Eventually, all these measures were accorded theological respectability in Aquinas' *Summa*. Although Aquinas did not deal specifically with witchcraft, he expressly condemned both implicit and explicit pacts with the devil. "[Aquinas' work] was the crucial link that allowed the Inquisition to shift its attention from outright heretics to magicians and sorcerers, and inquisitors often cited Aquinas between 1323 and 1327 when attacking the invocation of spirits as heresy."[23] The *Summa* also approved of punishment as a spiritual good. The Inquisition thus gained both theoretical and moral justification.

The Inquisition took witchcraft seriously, which led the people to believe in its reality. Edward Burman observes that the combination of inquisitorial efficiency and the adoption by the secular courts of inquisitorial techniques embedded the reality of witchcraft in the European consciousness.[24] "The church created the elaborate concept of devil worship and then used the persecution of it to wipe out dissent, subordinate the individual to authoritarian control, and openly denigrate women."[25] "The separate Dominican streams of violent physical repression and theological argument merged in the inquisitorial persecution of witchcraft. . . . The power and guile of the essentially Dominican antiwitch Inquisition helped to fix in the popular imagination an irrational concept that might otherwise have played a minor role in European history."[26]

By the end of the fourteenth century municipal courts had adopted inquisitorial techniques. Informers were no longer required to substantiate their accusations in these courts. Formerly, judicial procedure operated under the "talion"—a statute that demanded that any accuser who failed to convince a judge of the validity of his or her case suffer the same penalty that the accused would have suffered if found guilty.[27] Once the talion was abolished, accusations were facilitated, and the task of the inquisitors was more and more not to discover the truth but to elicit confessions. In fact, in 1578 inquisitor Francisco Peña declared that the main purpose of a witch's trial and execution was not the salvation of the accused's soul but the advancement of the public good. This was done by putting fear into the hearts of the onlookers.[28]

Christina Larner sees the era of the witch-hunts as a period of transition from restorative, interpersonal justice to abstract, rational, bureaucratic justice with repressive sanctions, marked by a "shift in responsibility from the accuser to the court official, which had the effect of making frivolous or vindictive accusation possible. . . . [This] system of abstract justice . . . made possible the victimless crime of simply being a witch, of being the servant of the Devil."[29]

There is also evidence that inquisitors became rich through the witch-hunts, which involved bribery and the confiscation of the accused's money and property. Some witches were even condemned posthumously, their bodies dug up and burned, and their heirs' property confiscated. The families of the accused were responsible for all expenses connected with the imprisonment, including food and clothing, and even whatever costs were connected with the execution.[30] "Victims were charged for the very ropes that bound them and the wood that burned them. Each procedure of torture carried its fee. After the execution of a wealthy witch, officials usually treated themselves to a banquet at the expense of the victim's estate."[31] In 1592 Father Cornelius Loos, who had accompanied many victims to the stake, observed: "Wretched creatures are compelled by the severity of the torture to confess things they have never done . . . and so by the cruel butchery innocent lives are taken; and, by a new alchemy, gold and silver are coined from human blood."[32] "The essential characteristics of what is commonly called witchcraft—a combination of *maleficium*, night-flights, sabbat, and pact with the Devil—were assembled in the period that ran from 1320–1486, and the Inquisition was responsible at least in part for this assemblage and for the great increase in witch trials at the end of the fifteenth century."[33]

In a period when any challenge to the church was seen as a challenge to society, the judges of both the secular courts and the inquisition believed they were acting as God's agents but many got carried away with ecclesiastical self-righteousness. Those accused of witchcraft were seen as rebels against church and state just at a time when the two were completely identified.[34]

THE VICTIMS

Even a skeptic like Robin Briggs, who takes great pains to point out that many of the victims of the witch craze were indeed men, goes on to observe: "It remains true that most accused witches were women."[35]

It becomes increasingly clear that the realities of popular life and belief do not accord at all with the official concept of witchcraft. The victims of the witch-hunts were *not witches* in the sense of the official demonologists' definition, although once subjected to torture many victims may have come to believe in the witch-hunter's definition of themselves as night-flying witches in pact with Satan.[36]

The traditional teaching of Christianity was that women were oversexed, rationally and morally inferior to men, and spiritually deficient. "The church, having sown the wind in its teaching about women, was now reaping the whirlwind." Sanctity was attributed to men, witchcraft to women.[37] Late medieval sermons, as well as popular stories and songs, denounced women's "slippery and manipulative" nature, betraying the misogynist tradition that lay at their roots.[38] Herbert Richardson notes that the period of witch persecutions coincided with the period of courtly love. "The Witch . . . was nothing other than the counterface of the Lady. She was the one who objectified all those anxieties and negative feelings that late medieval man could not allow to enter into his imagination and feelings about his Lady."[39] The witch was the one onto whom medieval man projected his fears of women.

By the 1500s the models of the female saint and the witch were virtually mirror images of each other. Each was possessed, the one by God, the other by Satan; each could read minds; each was capable of "flying," the one through levitation, the other through the air; each bore wounds, the one the stigmata, the other the so-called devil's mark. Each was, in her own way, a threat to ecclesiastical authority.[40]

Grace Jantzen also points to the developing capitalist economy which put men and women in competition with each other.[41] On the other hand, women who were poor, old, single, or widowed were seen as a drain on the resources of those involved in the developing economy. So, persecuting these women as witches acted as an important, gender-specific, method of social control.[42]

The witch in many cases was the poorest of the poor, dependent on her neighbors to stave off starvation. In the sixteenth century, . . . the poor were becoming poorer; more peasants were forced to beg or steal in order to survive. Old, single women, especially vulnerable to this economic crunch, came to be seen as nuisances. When they turned them down, people felt guilty, an uncomfortable state often exacerbated when the beggar cursed them for their refusal. Then when misfortune occurred, people turned on the beggars, a classic example of "blaming the victim."[43]

The most common victim was the old woman who resembled the Crone. "Common people of pre-reformational Europe relied upon wise women and men for the treatment of illness rather than upon churchmen, monks or physicians."[44] Wise women combined knowledge of medicinal herbs and pleas for divine assistance; thus, they offered medicine that was both more affordable and more effective than that offered by church-licensed physicians. "Denied the ancient role of clergy or the newly emerging one of doctor, women drew on their own networks of information and skills inherited from their mothers to serve as privileged counselors and practitioners."[45] Orthodox Christians, however, were taught that such healing was evil since health was to be left in God's hands and so the role of the healer became suspect.

The church branded anyone with knowledge of herbs as a witch. "Mere possession of herbal oils or ointments became grounds for accusation of witchcraft."[46] Midwives were also targeted. Childbirth was considered defiling, but the real "sin" of the midwives was easing the pains of childbirth, pains that had been divinely ordained as a result of Eve's "original sin."[47] No less an authority than Martin Luther had observed: "If [women] become tired or even die, that does not matter. Let them die in childbirth—that is why they are there."[48] As Helen Ellerbe notes, "It is hardly surprising that women who not only possessed medicinal knowledge but who used that knowledge to comfort and care for other women would become prime suspects of witchcraft."[49] Partly as a result of the witch-hunts, medicine became an exclusively male preserve and the Western tradition of herbal medicine was virtually destroyed.

The period of the witch trials marks the first time that women were criminalized on such a large scale. Usually, women's behavior had been considered the responsibility of the father or husband. Since, in patriarchal societies, men determined who was a "good woman," anyone deviating from their standards was vulnerable to charges of witchcraft as were any who exhibited "male" characteristics, like independence or aggression, or those who failed to fulfill female roles by remaining unmarried or, when married, by not bearing children. "The stereotype witch is an independent adult woman who does not conform to the male idea of proper female behaviour. She is assertive; she does not require or give love (though she may enchant); she does not nurture men or children, nor care for the weak. She has the power of words—to defend herself or to curse."[50] So, the same patriarchal misogyny that gave men leave to beat their wives ultimately sanctioned the torture and execution of thousands of "witches."

As for the status of women in European legal history, one notable fact about them is their absence. Until the sixteenth century, women made up a very small number of the defendants, accusers, or witnesses in legal cases. . . . Then around 1560 European secular courts began to hear accusations of witchcraft and sexual crimes, and women began to appear in court in large numbers, an entirely new phenomenon. . . . in the process of bringing these offenses under their jurisdiction, sixteenth-century courts were forced to admit their perpetrators to a new legal standing. . . . That European women first emerged into full legal adulthood *as witches*, that they were first accorded independent legal status in order to be prosecuted for witchcraft, indicates both their vulnerability and the level of antifeminism in modern European society.[51]

Unlike the Anabaptist martyrs, whose letters and theological tracts fill the pages of *Martyrs' Mirror,* the victims of the witch-hunts died leaving behind virtually no written records. One letter, however, does survive, written in 1590 by Rebecca Lemp to her husband. "Oh, husband, they take me from thee by force. How can God suffer it? My heart is nearly broken. Alas, alas! My poor dear children orphaned. Husband, send me something that I might die or I must expire under torture. If thou canst not today, do it tomorrow. Write to me directly. R. L."[52]

The torture which Rebecca Lemp feared so much was indeed horrifying. After being stripped, shaved, and searched with needles for the "mark of the devil," which could be any wart or birthmark, the accused witch was tortured in order to obtain the necessary confession. In addition to the mask of shame, the dressmaker's collar, and the ducking stool, women accused of witchcraft faced unbearable pain inflicted by thumb and leg screws, the iron maiden, and head clamps. *Gresillons* crushed the tips of fingers or toes in a vice; the *échelle*, or rack, violently stretched the body; while the *strappado* jerked the body in mid-air. The witch-chair was a seat of spikes which could be heated from below. Should a woman be strong enough to withstand the first round of torture, a second, more intense, session followed. The few who still held out were subjected to the "third degree" of torture that usually ended in death.[53]

Women convicted of witchcraft were usually burned to death. In 1197 Pedro II of Aragon had decreed that relapsed heretics should be burned; in 1198 Innocent III extended this mandate to include heretics who were not affected by excommunication. Once witchcraft was looked upon as heresy, this tradition of burning heretics turned against the accused witches. Why fire? Perhaps by burning the witches, those in power hoped to reduce the sorcery these women were accused of to ashes. Jeffrey Russell suggests that the choice of fire "is explained on the deepest levels by the purificatory power attributed to that element in most mythologies, and in Christianity the choice was reinforced by the analogy with hell and by the numerous examples of purificatory fire in the Old and New Testaments."[54]

That this torture was carried out in the presence of large crowds often numbering in the thousands gave it a ritual meaning beyond that of simple punishment. As a public purging of evil, it declared that the land was rid of demonic enemies and that not a trace of their hated presence remained. Once the condemned had been reduced to ashes, those very ashes would be thrown in the wind or scattered over moving water. But public witch executions were more even than a purging: they affirmed that the ruler who ordered them was godly, and even more important, that his power was greater than the forces of evil.[55]

In other words, the public burning of witches served to assure the people both that the power of the devil had, at least for the moment, been overcome, and that church and state were in safe, strong hands. The execution also sent a strong message to other women not to consort with midwives or healers, and even to fear and distrust all others of their sex.

THE *MALLEUS MALEFICARUM*

"By the end of the fifteenth century, a whole doctrine of witchcraft had been developed together with a technique of systematic persecution."[56] Two Dominican inquisitors, Heinrich Institor Kraemer and Jakob Sprenger, successfully sought a bull from Pope Innocent VIII authorizing them to root out witchcraft. Two years later, in 1486, they compiled the *Malleus Maleficarum*[57] (Hammer against the Witches), a handbook to guide those involved in the apprehension and conviction of witches. The bull from Innocent was printed before the text itself, thus adding papal weight to the volume. "What is most striking about the *Malleus* is its preoccupation with sexual functions and its vicious attack on women in general."[58]

The author's purpose was clear. Witchcraft was a vast and vile conspiracy against the Faith; it was on the increase; witches were depopulating the whole of Christendom; and, through the impotence of the secular courts, these creatures remained unpunished. The *Malleus* was written to demonstrate precisely what witches were doing, and how they could be stopped. It first establishes the truth of the existence of witchcraft and its heretical nature; then elucidates the principal evils practised by witches and demons; and finally lays down formal rules for initiating legal action against witches, securing their conviction, and passing sentences upon them.[59]

The arguments in the *Malleus* rested on three underlying beliefs. Witchcraft was real and it would be heresy to deny it. Demons constantly interfered with human life. And both witchcraft and demonic activity were allowed by God for God's own purposes. Furthermore, although Satan could work alone, he preferred to work through

The Torture of Christine Böffgen by Judge Franz Buirmann at Rheinbach, in 1631. From Hermann Löher, *Hochnötige Klage*, Amsterdam, 1676 [1896], p. 482, plate 7. Courtesy of the Division of Rare and Manuscript Collections, Cornell University Library.

The Burning of Three Witches at Derneburg (1555). Barstow, *Witchcraze*. Dover Pictorial Archives Series. Dover Publications, Inc.

witches, offering greater offense to God by usurping God's own creatures.[60] "When it was published, [the *Malleus*] carried on its ti-
tlepage the bold epigraph, *Haeresis est maxima opera maleficarum
non credere*, 'to disbelieve in witchcraft is the greatest of heresies.' It
was the exact opposite of the ruling of the Church in the Dark Ages.
Since the 9th century, the wheel had come full circle."[61]

The authors of the *Malleus* used many weighty sources, mainly Aristotle,
who provides both natural explanation and the logical structure of each
proposition; the Scriptures, which form the basis for all theological, mi-
raculous, and moral arguments; St. Augustine, whose assertions concerning magic and demonology are scattered broadcast throughout the text;
and St. Thomas Aquinas, who furnishes a synthesis of the other three major
sources.[62]

The *Malleus* used the scholastic method of the *Summa*, stating a
question, then giving arguments, and finally reaching conclusions.
The manual, by shifting the blame for sorcery onto women with ex-
aggerated and misogynistic force, "created the popular view of the
witch as a woman that survives today; in that respect it was truly a
seminal work."[63] Women, after all, having been formed from a bent
rib, were deficient and more given to carnal lust, and easily pro-
voked.[64] Although filled with circular arguments and essentially
flawed, the book was extremely influential.

The *Malleus* took the position that women were especially suscep-
tible to witchcraft because they were feebleminded, weak in faith,
and cursed with an almost insatiable sexual desire which led them
to lust for the devil. Men were urged to express their gratitude to God
for sparing them the degradation of being born female.

Witches were thought to have special powers over the sexual and reproduc-
tive functions. Moreover, they also were believed to have a dampening effect
upon male potency, though the authors of the *Malleus* hedge on the point
whether witches actually had the power to undermine male sexual capacity
(to the point of removing their genital organs) or whether such problems
were the result of a bewitching delusion or "glamour," as they called it. The
authors gave a theological rationale for their overwhelming stress on vene-
real functions: God permitted witches "more power over this act, by which
the first sin was disseminated," than over other human actions.[65]

Other parts of the *Malleus* detailed the correct procedures to be
followed in witchcraft trials, including the various forms of torture
which could be used to extract confessions. "The judicial process
advocated in the *Malleus* is inexorable; its inquisitorial procedures
were, theoretically, implacable; and technically there would appear
to have been no escape once a witchcraft accusation had been initi-

ated."[66] Barbara Roberts has observed that the scientific revolution relied on the techniques of the Inquisition in the witch interrogations. Francis Bacon advised "teasing" or "torturing" the secrets out of Mother Earth.[67] Dominican Matthew Fox, who subtitles the *Malleus*, "How to Burn a Witch," characterizes the handbook as a "pure study of repression and projection," reflecting men's fears of sexuality, of the dark, and of women.[68] "The *Malleus Maleficarum* is an unsurpassed revelation of the primal anxiety about women that lurks in the heart of every man."[69] "It would not be far-fetched to describe the book as a cross between a scholastic work and a pornographic magazine."[70]

The production of manuals like the *Malleus* undoubtedly increased the likelihood of trials. Larner has pointed out that Mainz and Bamberg, two cities where the most numerous trials occurred, were early centers of printing.[71]

CONCLUSION

The witch craze has been described as "the shocking nightmare, the foulest crime and deepest shame of western civilization."[72] And yet, left alone, peasant societies would never have engendered such a phenomenon. "For centuries the wise women and other healers who worked on the frontiers of magic had existed side by side with the Church even in moments of tension."[73] It was the institution of the inquisitorial procedure and the extensive trials in both ecclesiastical and secular courts that transformed the beliefs of the people concerning witches into a "highly effective means of social control."[74]

Why did the witch craze last so long? Russell speculates:

the most fundamental reason for the longevity of witchcraft may be that, after the terrors of the fourteenth century made the image of the witch more vivid than ever before, the political power of the prince and the popes, the procedures of the Inquisition, the harsh strictures of canon and civil law, and the opinions of the theologians united to fix that vivid picture in the European mind almost indelibly.[75]

The peak of the witch craze came as Europe was in a period of transition, a time Burman has described as the "maximum moment of wrenching between a medieval world-view and that of a recognizably modern Europe, between the years 1570 and 1630."[76]

Just as there seems to be no one cause for the eruption of the witch craze, so there is no one reason for its decline. Factors most commonly cited include the weakening power of both Catholic and Protestant clergy; the rise of nationalism; and the development of the scientific method. Jantzen adds another factor, namely, a seventeenth-century change in gender ideology "which would affect the social control of women without any need to have recourse to witch persecutions."[77]

Prior to the period of the witch trials, women had been viewed as largely passive. But accusations of witchcraft required active women, "capable of entering into a devious and passionate relationship with the devil, and able to be a threat to people around her, and, in the eyes of the inquisitors, so great a danger to the church that no method of torture and extermination was too extreme."[78]

In the pre-industrial economy, however, it suited men's purposes better to reassert women's passivity. If women were once again viewed as weak and incapable of reasoning or moral decision making, they could more easily be restricted to the home and the needs of the children. This meant, however, that they could not at the same time be cunning, active witches, so the persecutions ended, at least in part, due to "the new gender construction resting on the infantilisation of women."[79]

Even the emerging scientific method was expressed in gendered terms. Bacon observed that philosophy, which was masculine, had the task of penetrating the secrets of nature, understood as feminine. Where the masculine was active, virile, and generative, the feminine was passive, weak, and waiting.

To say that it was the rise of science by itself which discredited belief in witches is too simple. The combination of new economic patterns, new religious structures, and the new "masculine" science all worked together to develop a new variety of the social control of woman, based on her passivity and inferiority. It can hardly be insignificant that the witch hunts ceased just when they were no longer necessary as a means of asserting male dominance.[80]

The role of the church must also be acknowledged. Much of what was done was done "with the permission of God," a phrase used whenever other arguments proved inconsistent or implausible. "It is an argument favoured by Catholic theologians and Reformers alike; and it reveals a colossal arrogance on the part of those who believe that their vapid subtleties really do elucidate the most intimate divine purposes which they alone fully comprehend. It is impossible to argue rationally against those who have been taken entirely into God's confidence."[81]

It took over 200 years of terror and death but the church finally transformed the image of paganism into devil worship and folk culture into heresy. The ancient celebrations of the earth goddess eventually became civil carnivals presided over by men. "No monuments have been built to their memory. Only a few relics, like the witch's cart, remain to mark their passing."[82] Six generations of children watched as their mothers burned at the stake, and the effects of the burning times are still with us. Women still struggle to find their voice, to tell their story, to proclaim their truth.

Scholars debate over the how and the why of the "witch craze," alternately exonerating or condemning the Inquisition, subscribing to or denying the impact of natural disasters like the Black Death, estimating and re-estimating the actual number of executions, until library shelves are filled with volumes and readers are left shaking their heads. Underlying all these opinions, however, is the grim reality that, between the fourteenth and seventeenth centuries women died apparently just for being women. It is a macabre and terrible period in the history of Western Christianity, and one that must not be forgotten.

NOTES

1. Helen Ellerbe, *The Dark Side of Christian History* (San Rafael, CA: Morningstar Books, 1995), pp. 137–138.

2. Hugh R. Trevor-Roper, "Witches and Witchcraft: An Historical Essay (II)," *Encounter* 28 (1967), pp. 16–17.

3. "The Burning Times," Part Two of the series, *Women and Spirituality*, video produced by The National Film Board of Canada, 1990.

4. Robin Briggs, *Witches & Neighbors: The Social and Cultural Context of European Witchcraft* (New York: Penguin Books, 1996), p. 6.

5. Anne Barstow speculates that the Black Death actually prevented an outbreak of witchcraft accusations in the fourteenth century by "almost providentially killing off" Europe's excess population. When conditions worsened in the sixteenth century and no such plague occurred, the people needed some other means for resolving tensions, namely, witchcraft accusations. Anne Llewellyn Barstow, *Witchcraze: A New History of the European Witch Hunts* (San Francisco: Pandora, 1994), p. 100.

6. Jeffrey Burton Russell, *Witchcraft in the Middle Ages* (Ithaca: Cornell University Press, 1971), pp. 169–170.

7. Caroline Walker Bynum, *Holy Feast and Holy Fast: The Religious Significance of Food to Medieval Women* (Berkeley: University of California Press, 1987), p. 262.

8. Julio Caro Baroja, "Witchcraft and Catholic Theology," in Bengt Ankarloo and Gustav Henningsen, eds., *Early Modern European Witchcraft: Centres and Peripheries* (Oxford: Clarendon Press, 1993), p. 26. The *Canon Episcopi* appeared in a work entitled *De ecclesiasticis disciplinis* by Regino, abbot of Prüm in Germany, who died in 915.

9. Margot Adler, *Drawing Down the Moon* (New York: Beacon Press, 1979), p. 49.

10. Baroja, "Witchcraft," pp. 27–28.

11. Stuart Clark, "Inversion, Misrule and the Meaning of Witchcraft," *Past and Present* 87 (May 1980), pp. 105, 118.

12. Richard Kieckhefer, "The Holy and the Unholy: Sainthood, Witchcraft, and Magic in Late Medieval Europe," *Journal of Medieval and Renaissance Studies* 24 (Fall 1994), p. 355.

13. Kieckhefer, "Holy and the Unholy," p. 359.

14. Christina Larner, *Witchcraft and Religion: The Politics of Popular Belief* (Oxford: Basil Blackwell Publisher Ltd., 1984), p. 3.

15. Grace M. Jantzen, *Power, Gender and Christian Mysticism* (New York: Cambridge University Press, 1995), p. 269.

16. Ellerbe, *Dark Side*, p. 121.

17. John Tedeschi, "Inquisitorial Law and the Witch," in Ankarloo and Henningsen, eds., *Early Modern European Witchcraft*, p. 85.

18. Edward Burman, *The Inquisition: The Hammer of Heresy* (New York: Dorset Press, 1984), p. 16. Much of the history of the Inquisition in this section is drawn from Burman.

19. Burman, *Inquisition*, p. 17.

20. Jantzen, *Power, Gender*, p. 246.

21. Burman, *Inquisition*, p. 34.

22. Church law had been collected into five books edited by Raymond Peñafort in 1234. Book V, *De Haereticus*, contained the principal constitutions of the Inquisition. Boniface, in the "sixth book," added all the later bulls.

23. Burman, *Inquisition*, p. 123.

24. Burman, *Inquisition*, p. 127.

25. Ellerbe, *Dark Side*, p. 114.

26. Burman, *Inquisition*, pp. 124–125.

27. Jantzen, *Power, Gender*, p. 268.

28. Ellerbe, *Dark Side*, p. 76.

29. Larner, *Witchcraft and Religion*, pp. 59–60.

30. Ellerbe, *Dark Side*, p. 80.

31. Barbara Walker, *The Woman's Encyclopedia of Myths and Secrets* (San Francisco: Harper & Row, 1983), p. 1086.

32. Russell Hope Robbins, *The Encyclopedia of Witchcraft and Demonology* (New York: Bonanza Books, 1981), p. 16.

33. Burman, *Inquisition*, p. 117.

34. Russell, *Witchcraft*, p. 3.

35. Briggs, *Witches & Neighbors*, p. 261.

36. Richard A. Horsley, "Who Were the Witches? The Social Roles of the Accused in the European Witch Trials," *Journal of Interdisciplinary History* 9, no. 4 (Spring 1979), p. 712.

37. Larner, *Witchcraft and Religion*, p. 61. See also M. G. Dickson, "Patterns of European Sanctity: The Cult of Saints in the Later Middle Ages" (unpublished doctoral dissertation, University of Edinburgh, 1974).

38. Rosemary Radford Ruether, *Women and Redemption: A Theological History* (Minneapolis: Fortress Press, 1998), p. 127. See also Mary Potter Engel, "Historical Theology and Violence against Women: Unearthing a Popular Tradition of Just Battery," in Mary Potter Engel and Walter E. Wy-

man, eds., *Revisioning the Past: Prospects in Historical Theology* (Minneapolis: Fortress Press, 1992), pp. 51–76.

39. Herbert W. Richardson, *Nun, Witch, Playmate: The Americanization of Sex* (New York: Harper & Row, 1971), p. 64.

40. Bynum, *Holy Feast*, p. 23.

41. Jantzen, *Power, Gender*, pp. 270–272.

42. Marianne Hester, *Lewd Women & Wicked Witches: A Study of the Dynamics of Male Domination* (London: Routledge, 1992), cited in Jantzen, *Power, Gender*, p. 274.

43. Barstow, *Witchcraze*, p. 26.

44. Ellerbe, *Dark Side*, p. 131.

45. Barstow, *Witchcraze*, p. 109.

46. Ellerbe, *Dark Side*, pp. 132–143. See also Jeanne Achterberg, *Woman as Healer* (Boston: Shambhala, 1991).

47. Many cultures considered childbirth defiling, due to the blood involved. Consequently, there are many rituals of purification prescribed for women following childbirth, for example, the Catholic custom of the "churching of women," an outgrowth of the Jewish rite of purification, performed forty days after the birth of a boy and eighty days after the birth of a girl.

48. Karen Armstrong, *The Gospel According to Woman: Christianity's Creation of the Sex War in the West* (New York: Doubleday, 1987), p. 69. It was also Luther who wrote that the witch should not be compared to the virgin but to the good wife, since, by being obedient to her husband, a woman would avoid the temptation to use magic. See Ruether, *Women and Redemption*, pp. 127–128.

49. Ellerbe, *Dark Side*, p. 136.

50. Larner, *Witchcraft and Religion*, pp. 62, 84.

51. Barstow, *Witchcraze*, p. 41.

52. "The Burning Times."

53. Hugh R. Trevor-Roper, *The European Witch-Craze of the Sixteenth and Seventeenth Centuries and Other Essays* (New York: Harper Torchbooks, 1967), pp. 120–121. See also "The Burning Times" and "Witches," an installment of the A&E series, *Ancient Mysteries*, 1996.

54. Russell, *Witchcraft*, pp. 150–151.

55. Barstow, *Witchcraze*, p. 143.

56. Hugh R. Trevor-Roper, "Witches and Witchcraft: An Historical Essay (I)," *Encounter* 28, no. 5 (May, 1967), p. 8.

57. Heinrich Kraemer and Jakob Sprenger, *Malleus Maleficarum*, Montague Summers, trans. (London: Pushkin Press, 1948).

58. Elizabeth Clark and Herbert Richardson, *Women and Religion: A Feminist Sourcebook of Christian Thought* (San Francisco: Harper San Francisco, 1977), p. 118.

59. Sydney Anglo, "Evident Authority and Authoritative Evidence: The *Malleus Maleficarum*," in Sydney Anglo, ed., *The Damned Art: Essays in the Literature of Witchcraft* (London: Routledge & Kegan Paul, 1977), p. 15.

60. Anglo, "Evident Authority," pp. 15–16. Anglo goes on to point out that "the whole argument for persecution rests upon a monstrous para-

dox, since witches are merely serving God's mysterious purposes." If God permits the devil to work evil through human agents, why aren't the witches praised instead of blamed?

61. Trevor-Roper, "Witches and Witchcraft," p. 15.

62. Anglo, "Evident Authority," p. 18.

63. Burman, *Inquisition*, p. 130.

64. Anglo, "Evident Authority," p. 16. Anglo notes that the "monkish misogyny of the *Malleus* is blatant."

65. Clark and Richardson, *Women and Religion*, p. 118. See *Malleus Maleficarum*, part 1, question 6 and part 2, question 1.

66. Anglo, "Evident Authority," p. 28.

67. Barbara Roberts, in "The Burning Times."

68. Matthew Fox, in "The Burning Times."

69. Clark and Richardson, *Women and Religion*, p. 120.

70. Jantzen, *Power, Gender*, p. 266.

71. Larner, *Witchcraft and Religion*, p. 57.

72. Robbins, *Encyclopedia*, p. 3.

73. Burman, *Inquisition*, p. 189.

74. Horsley, "Who Were the Witches," pp. 713–714.

75. Russell, *Witchcraft*, p. 170.

76. Burman, *Inquisition*, p. 190. Horsley also notes the difficult transition from one economic-political system to another, a transition that enabled the authorities to induce the peasants to blame their troubles on "witches." By attacking these witches, society was able to unburden itself of troublesome elements. Horsley, "Who Were the Witches," p. 714.

77. Jantzen, *Power, Gender*, p. 274.

78. Jantzen, *Power, Gender*, p. 275.

79. Jantzen, *Power, Gender*, p. 275.

80. Jantzen, *Power, Gender*, pp. 275–276.

81. Anglo, "Evident Authority," p. 21.

82. "The Burning Times."

4

The Nuns of Port-Royal:
A Reform Movement Entangled
in Controversy

It is a tragic paradox that this monastery where the restoration of the Cistercian rule of perpetual silence was a major item on the reform program, this community whose vocation was to listen in silence to the silently spoken Word, was finally destroyed by torrents of words: words printed and spoken, words of debates in which the nuns had no part but upon which they were forced to take a stand, words which they in turn poured out in their defense. This paradox alone—a Cistercian solitude transplanted into Parisian society, the silent music of contemplation destroyed by endless polemic and debate—is perhaps enough to explain the failure of a reform that began with so much fervor and promise.[1]

PROLOGUE

Guidebooks describing popular sites in Paris seldom even list Port-Royal among the city's attractions, a sign perhaps of just how complete was its ultimate rejection and destruction. Some travel books, however, not only mention Port-Royal; they acknowledge its importance in French religious history and suggest it as a sort of "pilgrimage" stop for the tourist exploring the Left Bank.[2] Perhaps Louis XIV, who was responsible for the destruction of one of the monasteries by that name, would be dismayed to realize that Port-Royal has given its name to a métro stop on one of the busiest commuter lines in the city.

F. Ellen Weaver, one of the preeminent American authorities on Port-Royal, described her first visit to the Paris site, now a busy maternity hospital:

Inside the little seventeenth century church, with its beautifully balanced proportions at once enhanced and muted by the stark whitewash and spare furnishings, the busy boulevards seemed far away. The silence of the centuries filled the classic dome, and Port-Royal reasserted itself. As the chaplain of the hospital led me out into the cloister, he gestured toward the plain stone arches and exclaimed, "L'austerité janséniste!" "Cistercienne!" was my reflexive rejoinder. His shocked glance reminded me that this is not a common view. It was, however, the view of Mère Angélique and the nuns who lived there.[3]

According to Weaver, Port-Royal de Paris was designed by Antoine le Pautre, a leading seventeenth-century architect, who conceived it as a "little baroque gem" that Mère Angélique modified in order to make of it a Cistercian abbey church.[4] Even le Pautre's relatively modest design was too ornate for her. Bernard Dorival, a Parisian art critic, observed that "Poverty was of such importance in the spirituality of Port-Royal that the idea penetrated the art it commissioned." Dorival noted that the modifications which Mère Angélique directed le Pautre to make could be "summarized in two words: suppression and simplification."[5]

At least one contemporary found Mère Angélique's "innovations" singular and novel, while le Pautre himself apparently thought she was motivated by a desire to save money. What they and others like them failed to remember was Port-Royal's roots in the Cistercian reform, a reform marked by a spirit of poverty and simplicity of spirit. "As the Cistercians modified the Romanesque architecture and developed a pure and noble style expressive of simplicity, evangelical poverty, and prayer, the nuns at Port-Royal achieved a modification of the prevailing baroque of their era which expressed their serious piety."[6]

For good or ill, the history of Port-Royal, and the lives of the heroic women who inhabited it during this period, will forever remain inextricably interwoven with the complex period following the Reformation and Trent, the so-called Catholic Reformation, the period of the Cistercian monastic reform and, in France, the period of Jansenism.

HISTORICAL BACKGROUND: TRENT AND THE COUNTER-REFORMATION

By the 1530s all of Scandinavia and the British Isles, as well as much of Germany, France, and Austria, had been lost to Rome. Luther had asked that a general council examine his doctrines but nothing happened until 1545. The delay was politically motivated: the pope was caught between the Hapsburgs and the king of France. There was also real fear that the office of pope might be abolished if conciliarism, that is, the theory that a general council was superior to the pope, was allowed to win the day. It must also be acknowledged that the church was simply slow to recognize the seriousness of the Protestant movement and to appreciate just how deep the doctrinal disputes really went.[7]

In 1534 Pope Paul III took real steps to eliminate abuses within the church. In 1545 the Council of Trent opened, although it was attended by fewer than 40 bishops, and most of them were Italian. The council's impact was truly disproportionate to its size. "Until Vatican II, twentieth-century Catholicism was shaped more by the Council of Trent than by any other historically tangible event or force."[8]

As a result of the attacks made by Luther and Zwingli on the Mass, but also as a consequence of the generally widespread discontent on the part of Catholics with the chaotic state of liturgy and the liturgical books, Trent felt bound to keep a watchful eye on the process of reform.

By 1546 a uniform Latin text of the Bible, the Vulgate, had been produced, but the council, which wanted no liturgical "loopholes," realizing that it could not produce the necessary liturgical books, handed the task over to the pope, thus in effect ceding to the pope and the Curia the exclusive right of jurisdiction in liturgical matters. The period of episcopal independence in liturgical matters which had stretched back to the early days of the church was thereby, first in principle and then in practice, brought to an end. The appearance of the word *Romanum* in the titles of the breviary and the missal epitomized the situation.[9]

In defining Catholic doctrine on faith and grace, Trent steered a middle course between Pelagianism, the belief that human effort is everything, and the Protestant insistence that everything depends on God: the council taught that salvation is a free gift from God but requires human cooperation. The number and meaning of the sacraments were clarified; and for the first time, marriage required a priest and two witnesses.

Trent also created the Index of Forbidden Books mentioned in Chapter 2 and established seminaries. According to McBrien, both of these measures were considered temporary, and yet both endured and had a lasting effect on the life of the church. "The first kept both the laity and the clergy separated from the major intellectual works of modern times, and the second tended to sharpen the distinction between clergy and laity by encouraging an academic and spiritual formation for priests in isolation from the ordinary workaday world of the rest of the People of God."[10]

In 1540 the Society of Jesus, founded by Ignatius of Loyola, was approved by Paul III. The Jesuits became synonymous with the Counter-Reformation and, as the order most identified with the papal office, it was the Jesuits who came into regular conflict with the Parisian Jansenists and the supporters of Port-Royal.

The spirituality of the Tridentine church[11] was still marked by practices denounced by the reformers, such as the veneration of the saints, the cult of Mary, and eucharistic devotions outside of mass. Pope Alexander VII in 1661 forbade any translation of the missal into the vernacular under pain of excommunication, so many ordinary people recited the rosary during mass. Eucharist, surrounded as it was by mystery, by processions, by the practice of the forty hours devotion, and by benediction, was looked upon as an object of worship rather than a source of spiritual nourishment. "The liturgy became as much a grand spectacle as an act of community worship."[12]

THE CHURCH IN FRANCE AND GALLICANISM

"Gallicanism" (so-called because of its French, or Gallic, origins) is the term used to describe the concept that a national church, in particular the church in France during the fifteenth through seventeenth centuries, could challenge the authority of the pope. Some scholars differentiate three types of Gallicanism: political Gallicanism that pits the pope against the king or parliament; episcopal Gallicanism that refers to the relationship between the pope and the bishops of a country; and theological Gallicanism that places the authority of the general council and the local church above that of the pope.[13]

French bishops resisted the papal doctrine of infallibility, the "assertion that the pope was the final authority in matters pertaining to doctrine . . . [an assertion] intended to increase Rome's power over the Church and to prevent quarrels from further weakening the Church after the shattering impact of the Reformation."[14] The bishops claimed that their offices came from God through the apostolic succession and not from the pope. They therefore had both the right and the duty to define doctrine in their dioceses and to help to do so for the universal church through general councils.[15]

Traced by scholars to the fourteenth century quarrels between the French king Philip the Fair and Pope Boniface VIII, theological Gallicanism claimed for France the right to resist all but very restricted forms of papal intervention within its jurisdiction. French kings had controlled the papacy in Avignon from 1303–1377. The Great Schism of 1378–1417 was only concluded when the Council of Constance (1414–1417) declared the supremacy of general councils over popes (conciliarism) and removed the three papal claimants.[16] The state courts, the *parlements*, basing themselves on a royal ordinance, the so-called Pragmatic Sanction of Bourges (1438), interpreted this right of resistance rigorously.[17] In short, Gallicanism "favored conciliar ecclesiastical government to papal supremacy, the temporal independence of kings to papal pretensions of universal authority, and French usages and customs in general to anything which came from 'over the mountains.'"[18]

Even after Trent, Gallicanism persisted. The classical expression of theological Gallicanism may be traced to J. B. Bossuet, bishop of Meaux, who led the Assembly of the Clergy of France to publish the Four Gallican Articles of 1682 during the reign of Louis XIV. These articles included: (1) the rejection of the extreme parliamentary position that denied any papal intervention in temporal matters; (2) the admission of papal authority but only subject to conciliar supremacy; (3) the demand that popes respect the ancient customs and canons of the French church; and (4) the admission of papal primacy in matters of faith but denial of papal infallibility apart from the consent of the universal church.[19] The articles were condemned by the pope in 1690 and withdrawn by the king and clergy in 1693, but they were widely taught in France until the eighteenth century. "Vatican II, in its teaching on the relations between church and state, on collegiality, and on the local church, may be said to preserve, though in a very different form, some of the concerns of the Gallican tradition."[20]

By the sixteenth century French Catholicism was remarkably vital but also marked by a moral and intellectual decadence. The church was enormously wealthy, its treasury accounting for more than a third of the national patrimony. Benefices were bestowed on courtiers: a two-year-old, Henry of Guise, was in charge of six abbeys. More than forty bishoprics were held by laymen, while the country clergy were poor and ignorant, and often kept concubines or were public drunks.[21]

JANSENISM AND PORT-ROYAL

Although the papacy was strong in the seventeenth century, post-Reformation doctrinal controversies were far from resolved. Areas of particularly heated dispute included human nature and how it was affected by original sin, the question of free will, and the meaning of grace. In the sixteenth century Michael de Bay of Louvain, also known as Michael Baius, had taught that grace, immortality, and freedom from concupiscence were given to us in creation. In other words, they were not "extra" gifts from God, and therefore what was lost to us in original sin were not supplemental characteristics but goods that were constitutive of our very human nature. This sort of thinking led naturally to a great stress on original sin.[22]

One of Baius' students at Louvain was Cornelius Jansen (1585–1638). Jansen, ordained bishop of Ypres in 1636, wrote a defense of Baius entitled *Augustinus*, in which he attacked Thomism and the theology of the Jesuits and argued that Augustine, not Thomas, was the true representative of Christianity. The work "became controversial because it seemed to contain ideas on grace and free will that were closer to Protestantism than to the Catholic tradition."[23] Five propositions were extracted from the book; these propositions emphasized the absolute necessity and irresistible character of grace, leading critics to conclude that the book was denying free will, promoting moral rigorism, and generating pessimism about the possibility of salvation. The propositions were condemned by Pope Innocent X in 1633. Pope Urban VIII placed the book, which was published two years after Jansen had died of the plague, on the Index, but Jansenism, with its theory of predestination and demand for a morally rigorous lifestyle, spread rapidly, especially in France.[24]

In the *Augustinus*, Jansen pits Aristotle, whom he describes as the arch-logician whose methods are completely unsuited to spiritual discussions, against Augustine, who appealed to the imagination and emotions as well as to logic. According to Augustine, all that is good in us is the result of God's grace, which enables us to live rightly and do good works. So, although Jansen was branded by many as little more than a "Calvinist," he actually retained the Catholic belief in both faith and good works as necessary to salvation. Jansen also held strongly to Augustine's *Civitas Dei*, that is, the visible church as the locus for the incarnation of the Redeemer. Since communion with that church was thus absolutely necessary for salvation, neither Jansen nor any of his followers ever thought of breaking with Rome.[25] "Regarded as an extreme but legitimate branch of the Catholic Reformation, Jansenism raised important questions about Catholic theology, papal authority in theological matters, and the relation of individual conscience to that authority."[26]

One of Jansen's most influential friends proved to be Jean du Vergier de Hauranne, another student at Louvain who, in 1620, was made abbot of Saint-Cyran, a Benedictine monastery in central France. Known almost universally thereafter as Monsieur de Saint-Cyran, de Hauranne became a champion of both Jansenist thought and the need for an immediate end to abuses within the Roman church. Saint-Cyran was particularly outraged by what he considered the laxity of the Jesuit approach to the Christian life. The Jesuits did, in fact, urge confessors to be more understanding. They saw French Catholics as both independent and tired of weighty dogmas and meaningless ceremonies. The Jesuit approach to revitalizing the church in France was to make whatever accommodations were necessary to lure people back to the confessional and the altar. Taking the other extreme position, Saint-Cyran eventually concluded that the only "safe" place for the just person was in the cloister. Accordingly, he refused a number of politically influential positions, opting instead to spend more time in study, prayer, and meditation. Some see here the influence of Pierre Bérulle, a cardinal, theologian, and spiritual writer. Bérulle had established the French Congregation of the Oratory for clerical education. He had also been involved in French foreign policy, seeking to form a Catholic grand alliance against the Protestants.[27] "The cardinal's devotional principles stressed the need for humility and self-abasement as an essential first step in the process of redemption." Since Saint-Cyran spent so much time with Bérulle, at least one author feels that the abbot's religious beliefs owe much more to the cardinal than to Jansen.[28]

In 1621 Saint-Cyran made the acquaintance of Mère Angélique of the monastery of Port-Royal and an enduring partnership was born. This partnership was to have far-ranging implications for them, for Port-Royal, and for the church in Paris and throughout France.

Port-Royal was founded for the Cistercian order in 1204 by Mathilde de Garlande in a "swampy unhealthy valley of the Yvette about eight miles southwest of Versailles."[29] The abbey did not become important until Jacqueline Marie Arnaud was made its abbess in 1602 at the age of eleven. In 1625 to get away from the unhealthful situation, Mère Angélique (as she was known in religion) purchased the building that would be called Port-Royal de Paris and moved her sisters there.

MÈRE ANGÉLIQUE DE STE. MADELEINE

Angélique was a member of the Arnaud family, who, over the course of seventy-five years, were the driving force behind Port-Royal; many of the Arnauds also figured prominently in the controversy between the Jansenists and the Jesuits. Angélique's father, Antoine, a lawyer attached to the Parliament of Paris, had lived through some precarious times because of his loyalty to Henry III and his failure to join the Catholic League. After Henry's assassination, the League resisted his Huguenot heir, Henry IV. Eventually, however, Henry IV's position was solidified and the danger passed. But Antoine was not particularly well off and his father decided that Antoine's and Catherine's daughters would have to be placed in convents.[30]

82

Noble Daughters

The Abbey of Port-Royal. Louise-Madeleine Cochin (1686–1767). *Abbaye de Port Royal des Champs, 1709.* Sceaux Ile de France. Photo courtesy of Lauros-Giraudon.

Angélique's initial entry into the monastery was thus motivated by economic considerations and she herself was apparently less than pleased with the decision. Although her parents did everything they could to see to her material comfort, she "preferred Plutarch's *Lives* to sacred texts, and she amused herself by entertaining guests from the world she was compelled to abandon."[31]

Six years after her entrance, however, Angélique heard a sermon by a visiting monk and experienced a remarkable conversion. She came to believe that her mission was to reform herself and the whole convent. Her reform program had as its goal the reimposition of the Cistercian rule at Port-Royal. When both the other nuns and her family objected, Angélique nearly gave up her resolve until she heard another sermon based on Matthew's assurance that those who are persecuted for righteousness will be blessed. Angélique began her reform in earnest, a reform that included a strict observation of cloister and a spirit of poverty and simplicity.

Sedgwick tells of the incident which finally convinced Angélique's family that her intentions deserved their respect. In September of 1609 Antoine, Catherine, and their oldest son visited Port-Royal.

Refused admittance, they were invited by their daughter into an ad-joining parlor, the only room where visitors were allowed. When she ignored her father's insistence that they be admitted to the building proper, he threatened never to see her again. In reply to one of her nuns, who scolded her for her harsh treatment of her parents, Angé-lique remarked that since they had not consulted her before making her a nun, she didn't have to consult them about living like one. The whole scene caused Angélique to faint and, when she recovered, her family acceded to her wishes.[32]

Angélique was eventually joined at Port-Royal by her sisters, Agnès, Anne-Eugénie, Marie de Saint-Claire, and Madeline de Saint-Christine. Agnès became her helper in the reform and to-gether they weathered the initial struggles. Many of the nuns were living comfortably, enjoying their own property, and frequently en-tertaining friends and families. Naturally, they did not welcome the announcement of a return to a strict Cistercian rule. "By forcing nuns without a vocation to leave the establishment and by admit-ting only those who believed themselves to be called to monastic life, Angélique and Agnès were able to create a community that con-formed to their ideals."[33]

Recognizing the need for proper governance, Angélique made a serious effort to make the office of abbess elective, an ancient mo-nastic right that had virtually disappeared as monasteries and con-vents were given over to the control of secular rulers. By 1630 Angélique achieved her goal; her position was now elective.

Angélique had originally worked closely with Dom Boucherat, the Cistercian abbot. After his death she successfully applied to the pope and had Port-Royal placed under the jurisdiction of the arch-bishops of Paris and Sens and the bishop of Langres, Sébastien Zamet, another reformer. It was Zamet who was ultimately respon-sible for the meeting between Angélique Arnaud and Saint-Cyran.

Zamet encouraged Angélique to leave the Cistercians and to make Port-Royal the nucleus of a new order, the Institute of the Holy Sac-rament, which Zamet wanted to establish in Paris. Zamet per-suaded Agnès Arnaud to write a special prayer for the new order. When the prayer was denounced as heretical, Zamet enlisted the aid of Saint-Cyran to defend it. Although the charge of heresy was with-drawn, the institute did not survive and in 1636 Port-Royal was placed under the sole jurisdiction of the archbishop of Paris. Angé-lique, describing these events, wrote: "this persecution . . . was so great that the Court became involved, and there we were described as visionary heretics; and some even went so far as to call us witches."[34] But the incident cast Saint-Cyran in the role of chief de-fender of Port-Royal and it wasn't long before Angélique sought him

Angélique Arnaud. Philippe de Champaigne (1602–1674). *Mère Angélique Arnaud, abbesse de Port-Royal.* Louvre, Paris. Photo courtesy of Lauros-Giraudon.

The Abbé de Saint-Cyran. Philippe de Champaigne (1602–1674). *Jean Duvergier de Hauranne, abbé de Saint-Cyran (1581–1643)*, 1646–1648. Chateau de Versailles. Photo courtesy of Lauros-Giraudon.

out as the nuns' spiritual director, an office she felt was essential to both the community and her reform.

Nigel Abercrombie, in analyzing Angélique's approach to reform, observes that the process was marked by the typical stages. He points to three administrative measures that were "normally indispensable" for a viable reform: placing the house under the jurisdiction of the ordinary; moving from the country into the town; and securing freedom to elect the abbess. These steps were necessary in order to avoid opposition from the Cistercians, to put the nuns within reach of educated clergy, and to guard against unsuitable royal nominees for the office of leadership.[35] When Port-Royal de Paris opened in 1625 the disadvantages of the increased cost of city life and the reduced space in choir and dining room were offset by the introduction into the life of the abbey of Zamet and Saint-Cyran.

If Angélique valued Saint-Cyran for his religious ideals, he learned simplicity and penitence from her. In Saint-Cyran, Port-Royal had found the spiritual director who would guide it through the period of reform. It was, however, also Saint-Cyran's connection with Jansenism and his hostile relationship with Cardinal Richelieu that were to bring dire, and finally disastrous, repercussions on Port-Royal.

Saint-Cyran's disputes with the Jesuits can be traced to 1626 when the abbot "became involved in a literary quarrel with a Jesuit scholar, Garasse," who had published a four-volume work, *Somme théologique*. Saint-Cyran published his own refutation, *Somme des fautes et faussetez principales contenues en la somme théologique du Père Garasse*, which, as the title implies, pointed to the numerous "mistakes" and "false notions" in Garasse's writing. In his work Saint-Cyran emphasized the inadequacy of human reason, which was naturally inclined toward evil. Faith alone was trustworthy. This distrust of reason was to become a hallmark of Jansenist thought.

Saint-Cyran eventually became associated with a group of men who became known as the *solitaires* of Port-Royal. Although their number never grew very large, it included some of the outstanding thinkers of the day, men like Blaise Pascal, Pasquier Quesnel, Pierre Nicole, and Jacques-Joseph Duquet, who had turned away from promising careers and important political connections in order to engage in prayer and meditation.

Through his writings, in which he championed local clergy over the regular orders, and through his approach to monastic reform, Saint-Cyran made enemies in high places. Besides the hostility between the abbot and the Jesuits, Saint-Cyran also began to look dangerous to his former friend, the powerful Cardinal Richelieu. Although Saint-Cyran wrote nothing of a specifically political nature, he did oppose Richelieu's anti-Hapsburg, pro-Swedish (Protestant) foreign policy during the Thirty Years' War. Many leaders of the French Counter-Reformation opposed a foreign policy which they thought sacrificed the interests of the Catholic reconquest of Europe to those of the Bourbon dynasty.[36] Since Richelieu already faced opposition to his foreign policy from a group known as the *dévots*, who demanded that politics be based on religious principles, and since Saint-Cyran was a leader of the *dévot* faction, the stage was set for a bitter confrontation.[37]

In addition to political disputes, Saint-Cyran and Richelieu engaged in theological arguments, most importantly over the issue of penitential discipline. Saint-Cyran believed that contrition was necessary for absolution, that is, that a sinner's attitude in confession really mattered. Furthermore, this contrition should be based on the love of God and manifest itself in true reform rather than springing from the fear of punishment. Richelieu, for his part, thought contrition was very rare and actually made confession unnecessary; for the majority of people, the best that could be hoped for was confession motivated by attrition—the fear of divine retribution. Even in this matter, however, there was, as Van Kley points out, a political dimension. Had Saint-Cyran's demand for true contrition actually been put into action, it "would have entailed the abandonment of Richelieu's 'sinful' alliance with Swedish, Dutch, and German Protestants in favor of an alignment with France's mortal enemies, the Catholic Hapsburgs."[38]

So Saint-Cyran had managed to alienate the Jesuits, the cardinal-minister of France, and even the king, who agreed with Richelieu's approach to penitence. Saint-Cyran was arrested in May of 1638 and imprisoned at Vincennes. "The charge brought against Abbé de Saint-Cyran was that he was a heretic who taught a penitential theology contrary to the principles of the Council of Trent." Nothing to support the charge was ever discovered, but Saint-Cyran remained in prison for four years.[39]

Through letters smuggled out by visitors, Saint-Cyran was able to continue as spiritual director to the nuns of Port-Royal. With an insight reminiscent of the Anabaptists, the abbot came to appreciate the opportunity for growth in faith that persecution gave him. In his cell he had complete solitude and time for meditation and reflection.

In December of 1642 Cardinal Richelieu died; Saint-Cyran was released from prison the following February. Returning to Port-Royal, he told the nuns he intended to defend the doctrine of contrition, but he died of a stroke in October of 1643.[40] His death brought to an end the first phase of Jansenism, a phase that had begun in

1609 when Angélique Arnaud literally closed the doors of Port-Royal to her own father.

JANSENIST CONTROVERSIES AT PORT-ROYAL

By 1649 when the Jansenist controversies began in earnest, the number of nuns at Port-Royal had grown so large that some of them had moved back to Port-Royal des Champs. They had also adopted a white habit with a scarlet cross on the scapular and included perpetual adoration in their constitutions, both legacies from the time of the *Institut du Saint-Sacrement*.[41]

On July 1, 1649, Nicolas Cornet, speaking at the Sorbonne, proposed five propositions as heretical, tacitly implying that they had been drawn directly from Jansen's *Augustinus*.[42] Antoine Arnaud countered that the statements were ambiguous and open to various interpretations, not all of which would be deemed heretical. Pope Innocent X finally condemned the propositions in the 1653 bull, *Cum occasione*, in which the pope attributed the statements to Jansen. After much writing and arguing on both sides, a second bull, *Ad sanctam beati Petri sedem*, was issued by Pope Alexander VII in 1656 affirming that the condemned propositions were contained in the *Augustinus*. Arnaud's reply to the bull contained his famous distinction between *droit* and *fait*. By *droit*, Arnaud meant that he acknowledged the pope's claim that the five propositions were heretical; but by *fait* he declared that the pope was simply wrong when he said the propositions could be found in the *Augustinus*.

After a period of relative calm, King Louis XIV of France, in 1661, tried to force the nuns to sign a formulary[43] condemning the five propositions and admitting that they could be found in the *Augustinus*. Although some accepted the "loophole" of Arnaud's *droit/fait* distinction, most of the nuns refused to sign. Sedgwick holds that since they knew the *Augustinus* was a work approved by Saint-Cyran, to sign the formulary would have meant a condemnation of Mère Angélique's trusted spiritual advisor.[44] When three years passed with no change in their stance, the archbishop of Paris transferred twelve of the nuns to other convents. In July of 1665 the twelve nuns who had signed were left at Port-Royal de Paris, which became an independent monastery, while the nuns who had refused to sign were kept at Port-Royal des Champs under police supervision and were deprived of the sacraments. A compromise was initiated by Clement IX in 1669 whereby Port-Royal des Champs regained its freedom and remained independent of the Paris monastery. This period of relative tranquillity came to be called the "Peace of the Church," and it remains a bright spot in the tragic history of Port-Royal. This was the time when some outstanding works, such as Blaise Pascal's *Pensées* and Saint-Cyran's *Considérations* were published.

Then, in 1679, the new archbishop of Paris, Harlay de Champvallon, on orders from Louis XIV, renewed the persecution of Port-Royal, forbidding the admission of new members and thus condemning the institute to slow extinction. In 1706 the nuns refused to sign the bull, *Vineam Dei*, and Louis XIV deported the twenty-two old nuns still living in the house. Two years later the king had the building destroyed; even the corpses in the cemetery were exhumed and reburied in a common grave.

Port-Royal was gone, but as Sedgwick notes, the "wanton destruction of Port-Royal had a detrimental effect on French culture. . . . The Enlightenment emerged phoenix-like from the ruins of Port-Royal, and the French culture as a whole was dangerously corrupted by the facile optimism of the philosophes and by their naive faith in the powers of reason and science."[45]

ANGÉLIQUE DE SAINT-JEAN ARNAUD D'ANDILLY

Angélique de Saint-Jean was the niece of Mère Angélique; she was the leader of the nuns who refused to sign the anti-Jansenist formulary and the historiographer of the monastery and the reform movement. Weaver describes Angélique de Saint-Jean as a fervent Augustinian, a determined ascetic, and an ardent defender of conscience and truth.[46] It was her very independence that compelled Angélique de Saint-Jean to challenge both the church, in its demand for a signature renouncing the alleged Jansenist statements, and the male leaders of Port-Royal who had found in Antoine Arnaud's distinction between *droit* and *fait* a way to compromise on the formulary.

In an intriguing article Weaver makes the case that this Angélique is actually a more complex and interesting person than her more famous aunt.[47] Angélique de Saint-Jean's life alternated between Port-Royal des Champs where she served as novice mistress, and Port-Royal de Paris where she worked on her *Mémoires* of Mère Angélique. She returned to Port-Royal des Champs in 1653 as subprioress but was in Paris again by the time of the 1661 order to sign the formulary. Angélique de Saint-Jean became the leader of the nuns who refused to sign.

Weaver makes use of Jean LeClerq's analysis of the growth of religious orders from reform to established tradition.[48] LeClerq delineates three significant persons in such a transformation: the "founder," the one who starts something new; the "subleader," the one who supports and perhaps continues the work of the founder;

and the "third superior," the one who, at some distance from the founder chronologically (and not necessarily "third" in the strict sense), stabilizes and organizes the now-reformed institute. In the case of Port-Royal, these roles were filled by Mère Angélique, Mère Agnès, and Angélique de Saint-Jean, respectively. Angélique de Saint-Jean was deeply influenced by her aunt by whom she had been educated from the age of six and she both admired and respected the ideals of Mère Angélique. Her letters indicate that she was closer emotionally to Mère Agnès but that she turned to Mère Angélique when she needed guidance.[49]

It was Angélique de Saint-Jean who took a firm stand against signing the formulary, who solidified Mère Angélique's campaign to restore the choice of abbess to election rather than regal nomination, and who continued her aunt's efforts to restore the Divine Office to its proper place in the life of the monastery.[50] It was to Angélique, too, that the task of obtaining papal approval of the revised *Constitutions* fell.

A gifted writer, Angélique de Saint-Jean used the theme of martyrdom as a paradigm for the nuns refusing to sign the formulary, wrote letters worthy of a theologian, and perhaps more than any other person, enshrined the memory of her aunt's life and work of reform in her memoir, *Relation sur la vie de la Révérende Mère Angélique*, a work that occupied Angélique de Saint-Jean on and off for nearly twenty years. Much of what is known about the difficult periods between 1661 and 1665–1669, when the nuns who refused to sign the formulary were first dispersed, then placed under interdict at Port-Royal des Champs, comes from her letters and her essay, "*Relation de la Captivité*."[51] Since Mère Angélique died in 1661, she escaped much of this turmoil; it was Angélique de Saint-Jean who led the community, held it together, at least for a time, and wrote its history or, some would say, its myth.[52] It was she who received the vows of the last nun to be professed at Port-Royal. Angélique de Saint-Jean, then, is not just "third superior," historian, biographer, and theologian; she is, indeed, the hero of the myth of Port-Royal.

Like her aunts and many of the other women who either joined or supported Port-Royal, Angélique de Saint-Jean exemplifies the tendency in post-Trent Catholicism to provide education for girls that was equal to that of boys. Indeed, most of the Jansenist women were very well educated, since Jansenist bishops were as serious about education as they were about reforming the moral and spiritual life.[53] While much that is written about this period emphasizes the theological disputes between the Jansenists and the Jesuits, the Jansenist attitude toward women is too important to overlook. Jansenists believed that all laity, including women, had the right to full participation in the liturgy and to access to the scriptures. Thus, "the Jansenist women reflect many of the characteristics of French Catholic culture of the age: a commitment to heightened levels of learning and serious spiritual renewal."[54]

In the monasteries, when the need arose, women took charge. "At Port-Royal when the priests who had been their spiritual directors went into exile, Mère Angélique de Saint-Jean Arnaud d'Andilly wrote a treatise on spiritual direction, which could have been called 'How to Do Without a Spiritual Director.' Her solution was for the abbess to become spiritual director . . . or for the individual nun to seek guidance in Scripture."[55]

There is an anecdote from this period which, although not directly connected to the story of Port-Royal, provides an echo of the Belgian Beguines of Chapter One. Noting that many of the Jansenist bishops established groups of laywomen in their dioceses, Weaver cites a description of such a group by Claude Lancelot:

They have no vows but those of their baptism . . . They have no cloister, but live in a manner similar to nuns. . . . They go to church in the parish. . . . They are engaged to establish little schools and to teach Christian doctrine to members of their sex throughout the diocese. . . . They sleep in dormitories. . . . They have a common room where they say the daily office. . . . They dress in secular clothing but very modestly, completely covering the lower arm.[56]

POSTSCRIPT: JANSENISM AND THE NEO-GALLICAN LITURGICAL REFORM MOVEMENT

The Neo-Gallican period extends roughly from 1670 when work began on the reform of the Paris breviary, to 1875 when Orléans became the last diocese in France to reinstate the Roman usage. The "Gallican" implies a return to the Carolingian reform of the Roman books in the early Middle Ages, but it would be more accurate to regard it as a designation pointing to a high regard for the autonomy of the local church vis à vis Rome, as indicated in the section on Gallicanism earlier in this chapter. Neo-Gallicans respected the bishop of Rome, but as a *primus inter pares*. This, unfortunately, clashed with the post-Trent emergence of a powerfully centralized papacy.

This is also the period in France of "*la grande siècle*," the age of Louis XIV, and the rise of absolutism. In the inevitable clashes between Rome and the king, particularly acute with Louis' insistence on the *régale* (royal control of the subsidies of vacant episcopal sees), it seems the French bishops were comfortable with supporting whichever side allowed them greater freedom.

The Neo-Gallican period also coincides with the age of classicism and humanism, and reflects to some extent the influence of the Enlightenment—the reformers believed passionately in their own competence and in the dignity of every member of the church. A further influence on the liturgists of this period was the advancement in biblical and patristic studies, particularly among the Benedictines of Saint Maur.

Although sweepingly dismissed by at least one powerful critic as "Jansenist,"[57] the Neo-Gallican books can actually be subdivided into groups: the "Orthodox," such as the Breviary of Rouen whose author, Urbain Robinet, was not in any way connected with Jansenism; the breviary of Cluny, a distinct and widely admired work; and the Neo-Parisian, most of whose authors were indeed "*Appellants*,"[58] but who were chosen by Archbishop Vintimille for their talent, despite their Jansenist connections.[59]

Weaver observes that it is difficult to prove or disprove the charge that these reformed books are specifically "Jansenist," since most of the liturgists of the day were either directly connected to Port-Royal or were sympathetic to, and believers in, the same principles of reform.[60]

What were those principles? Perhaps the key to their articulation is the overriding conviction that the liturgy had to be accessible to all Christians, not just clerical specialists,[61] and that nothing should be used in the church's public worship that lacked proper "authority," that is, nothing not found in scripture or in the authentic writings of the church fathers. Neo-Gallicans gave priority to Sunday over all other feasts. They classified some feasts while eliminating others in an attempt to simplify the calendar. Legendary readings were eliminated from the office, responsories and antiphons were all taken from scripture, and the hymnal was reformed.

As indicated earlier, Trent had left the reform of the liturgical books to the pope, and this was accomplished first in Pope Paul V's *Breviarium Romanum* and *Missale Romanum* (Roman Breviary and Roman Missal). There was also a papal attempt at calendar reform. The Tridentine usage, however, was not a blending of Roman usage with local customs but represented the usage of the Roman church exclusively. The very early centuries represented all that was good; any subsequent additions or revisions could and should be destroyed.

The French bishops, however, were able to take advantage of the stipulation in the bull, *Quod a nobis*, which exempted from compulsory implementation of the Roman books any dioceses which had local usages going back more than 200 years. The *Breviarium Parisiense* of 1680 was the first book not to bear the formula, "*ad for-*

mam sacrosancti concili Tridenti restitutum" (in the restored form of the holy council of Trent).

The Neo-Gallican tendency to use every part of the mass or the office in order to produce a harmonized presentation of the feast at hand can be criticized as overly didactic, but it must remembered that one of their goals was to remove the "mystery" from the church's worship. Mystery, they felt, may have been justified when Christianity existed in the midst of paganism, but it had no place in modern society.[62]

The very autonomy which inspired the Neo-Gallican reform accounted ultimately for its demise. Although a few of the books, notably those of Rouen, Cluny, and Paris, were used as models, it is nevertheless true that each diocese had its own usage. After the Revolution the dioceses were reduced in number by the simple step of making them coterminous with the civil départements. Liturgical diversity became liturgical chaos and the Roman usage was reinstated throughout France.

There is a telling anecdote about a response to Louis XVIII's reinstatement of the Roman books in the chapel royal in Paris. An anonymous author observed that, even if the French books did demonstrate better taste in hymns, lessons chosen more carefully, and a great overall ingenuity of arrangement, still, unity of practice was more important. In reply a second anonymous writer questioned why, if that were the case, unity had to entail the sacrifice of the better books.

It was this desire for "unity" (read "Roman control") that seemed to lie behind Guéranger's critique. But, in the name of that unity, he attacked not only the work of the reformers, but also their very character and intentions. He praised the role of Charlemagne while condemning that of Louis XIV. And he did so with reference to an ancient unity of practice which even he admitted never existed. And, at least until Vatican II, Guéranger carried the day.

Liturgical scholars today, however, are increasingly aware of the positive contributions of the Neo-Gallicans, Jansenist or not. Theodore Klauser makes a telling observation:

It was the movements of Jansenism, Gallicanism, and th Enlightenment, disapproved of as they were by the Church and for the most part condemned as a body for being deviationary, which, just like the Reformation in the sixteenth century, detected some fundamental weaknesses in liturgical practice and were concerned to eliminate them. From a diversity of motives, they proposed that the liturgy should be simplified and that its main ideas should be better worked out. In a variety of ways, they attempted also to bring the faithful to participate intelligently in its celebration.[63]

And Weaver herself concludes that, because of "the care the authors took to draw on the treasures of scripture and the early Christian writers for the composition of liturgical texts that were literary gems as well as instruments of theological instruction," the Neo-Gallican liturgies are indeed worth revisiting.[64]

CONCLUSION

Port-Royal's mission . . . was to rekindle faith (after a century of incredulity) by its exemplary piety, in order to prevent Christendom from being overwhelmed by the rising tide of secularism. The Jansenists seemed almost to foresee the Enlightenment, with its emphasis on human, rather than divine, capabilities, and they warned their contemporaries that the heavenly city was in danger, but ironically, instead of strengthening its foundations, Bishop Jansen and his supporters unwittingly opened the gates of the city to the philosophes.[65]

Port-Royal des Champs lay in ruins; Port-Royal de Paris was in the hands of strangers. During the Revolution the building in Paris was renamed Port-Libre and turned into a jail housing political prisoners, a poetic irony in the light of all that the nuns had suffered at the hands of politicians. Later the site became an orphanage and, finally, the maternity hospital now found on the Boulevard de Port-Royal. In the Chevreuse Valley visitors may see the stubborn remains of the abbey that would not yield entirely to destruction. There is a small chapel and a museum lovingly maintained by the Society of Friends of Port-Royal. Here can be found a copy of the *Augustinus,* the death masks of Mère Angélique and Pascal, and copies of various portraits and archives.[66] The dream lies in ruins but it is hardly forgotten.

Many church historians have speculated that, had Trent occurred just a few decades earlier, the need for the Protestant Reformation may well have been obviated. It is one of the great "what if's" of western Christianity. And it tempts those who admire the work of Mère Angélique, Saint-Cyran, Mère Agnès, and Angélique de Saint-Jean to wonder "what if" there had been no Protestant Reformation. Perhaps then the theology and spirituality of Jansen and of Port-Royal could have been evaluated on their own merits and not have been seen as a further threat to an institution so recently and so deeply wounded by division.

Nor should we allow all the scholarly ink that has been spilled over the Jansenist influence at Port-Royal to obscure the fact that the nuns of the reform thought of themselves first and foremost as Cistercian in spirit. Fidelity to the Cistercian ideal marked many of the writings of the nuns of Port-Royal, and devotion to the rule of St.

Benedict as interpreted by the Cistercians was integral to the life of the monastery.

In 1707, when the few old nuns remaining at Port-Royal des Champs were making their last stand in the losing battle against the political and ecclesiastical forces bent on destroying them, they drew up many official acts and filled many journal pages with remonstrances of their innocence. Always they began by identifying themselves as "*Soeurs de l'abbaye de Port-Royal des Champs de l'Ordre de Cisteaux.*" Cîteaux may have disclaimed them, but they never ceased to consider themselves Cistercian.[67]

Mère Angélique, who began the reform, Mère Agnès, who was the principal writer of the *Constitutions* of the reformed abbey, and Angélique de Saint-Jean, who saw the reform through its most troubled period, all took great pains to preserve the spirit of the Cistercian reform of the Rule of St. Benedict. "The emphasis on poverty, the commitment to abstinence, the return to the practice of perpetual silence except for one period a day called *la conférence*, recognition of the role of the Holy Spirit in prayer—all of these were important means employed by the founders of Cîteaux to return to the *puritas Regulae*, and all of them are recorded in the *Constitutions de Port-Royal.*[68]

We will never know how things might have turned out had Port-Royal emerged under different circumstances but many of the documents and decisions of Vatican II have validated the concerns of the Jansenists in the areas of liturgy and scripture. Even the doors of theological academia have finally been opened to the laity, including women. While there is much in modern Western society that would be abhorrent to the moral sensibilities of our friends of Port-Royal, there is also much that would make them smile. The reform goes on.

NOTES

1. F. Ellen Weaver, *The Evolution of the Reform of Port-Royal: From the Rule of Cîteaux to Jansenism* (Paris: Éditions Beauchesne, 1978), p. 33.

2. See, for example, Giles Desmons, *Walking Paris: Thirty Original Walks In and Around Paris* (Lincolnwood, IL: Passport Books, 1997), p. 63.

3. Weaver, *Evolution*, p. 89.

4. Weaver, *Evolution*, p. 89.

5. Bernard Dorival, "*Le Jansénisme et l'Art Français,*" *Bulletin de la Société des Amis de Port-Royal* (1952), pp. 13–14.

6. Weaver, *Evolution*, p. 91.

7. Richard P. McBrien, *Catholicism: Study Edition* (New York: Harper & Row, 1981), p. 635.

8. McBrien, *Catholicism*, p. 635.

9. Theodore Klauser, *A Short History of the Western Liturgy*, Second Edition (Oxford: Oxford University Press, 1979), pp. 117–118.

10. McBrien, *Catholicism*, p. 636.

11. "Tridentine" refers to the organization of the Roman Catholic Church as it was defined by the Council of Trent, 1545–1563.

12. McBrien, *Catholicism*, p. 637.

13. See, for instance, Frederick J. Cwiekowski, "Gallicanism," in Joseph A. Komonchak et al., eds., *The New Dictionary of Theology* (Wilmington: Michael Glazier, Inc., 1987), p. 415.

14. Alexander Sedgwick, *Jansenism in Seventeenth-Century France: Voices from the Wilderness* (Charlottesville: University Press of Virginia, 1977), p. 10.

15. Sedgwick, *Jansenism*, p. 10.

16. See Chapter 2, Note 5.

17. Benedict M. Ashley, "Gallicanism," in Richard P. McBrien, ed., *The Harpercollins Encyclopedia of Catholicism* (San Francisco: Harper San Francisco, 1995), p. 553.

18. Dale Van Kley, *The Jansenists and the Expulsion of the Jesuits from France 1757–1765* (New Haven: Yale University Press, 1975), p. 30.

19. Ashley, "Gallicanism," p. 553.

20. Cwiekowski, "Gallicanism," p. 416.

21. Louis Cognet, *Post-Reformation Spirituality* (New York: Hawthorn Books, 1959), p. 56.

22. McBrien, *Catholicism*, p. 638. Baius' work represents a revolt against the Scholastic devotion to "reason," by which was meant the categories of Aristotle. The Scholastics attempted to explain every article of faith by determining its metaphysical equivalent. This, however, dissatisfied ordinary Christians, who were untouched by, and probably did not even understand, such abstract thinking. Baius and those like him were trying both to make reasonable concessions to the Reformation and to put theology back in touch with the masses. See St. Cyres, "Jansenism," in James Hastings, ed., *Encyclopedia of Religion and Ethics* (New York: Charles Scribner's Sons), p. 476.

23. Jansen, "Cornelius," in McBrien, ed., *Harpercollins Encyclopedia*, p. 687.

24. McBrien, *Catholicism*, p. 638.

25. St. Cyres, "Jansenism," p. 476.

26. W. David Myers, "Jansenism," in McBrien, ed., *Harpercollins Encyclopedia*, p. 687.

27. "Pierre de Bérulle," in McBrien, ed., *Harpercollins Encyclopedia*, p. 159.

28. Sedgwick, *Jansenism*, p. 21.

29. Eugen Lachenmann, "Port-Royal," in Samuel M. Jackson, ed., *The New Schaff-Herzog Encyclopedia of Religious Knowledge* (New York: McGraw Hill Book Company, 1967), p.121.

30. Alexander Sedgwick, "The Nuns of Port-Royal: A Study of Female Spirituality in Seventeenth-Century France," in Lynda L. Coon, Katherine J. Haldane, and Elisabeth W. Sommer, eds., *That Gentle Strength: Histori-*

cal Perspectives on Women in Christianity (Charlottesville: University Press of Virginia, 1990), pp. 176–177. Sedgwick notes that the initial application for papal approval of Angélique's appointment as abbess of Port-Royal was turned down because she was too young, but that a second application was sent asserting that she was seventeen when she was actually eleven. That application was approved in 1601.

31. Sedgwick, "Nuns," p. 178.

32. Sedgwick, "Nuns," p. 179. The Jansenists would later refer to this day, September 25, 1609, as "The Day of the Grating." See Marc Escholier, *Port-Royal: The Drama of the Jansenists* (New York: Hawthorn Books, Inc., 1968), pp. 10–12.

33. Sedgwick, "Nuns," p. 181.

34. Quoted in Sedgwick, "Nuns," p. 182.

35. Nigel Ambercrombie, "Mère Angélique and Port-Royal," *The Downside Review* 68 (July 1950), pp. 346–347.

36. Van Kley, *Jansenists*, p. 11. Another important event in French history that also coincided more or less with the appearance of Jansenism was the Fronde, a sort of civil war that resulted from the eruption of long-standing tensions between the royal government and the parliament of Paris. Facing the paradox of both holding their offices from the king and fearing the increasingly powerful position of the king, many *parlementaires* adopted an attitude of reserve toward social life and functions, a sort of rejection of the "world" that was one characteristic of extreme Jansenism. Some scholars see an intrinsic connection between Jansenism and the Fronde, but that is an oversimplification. See Van Kley, *Jansenists*, pp. 19–20.

37. Sedgwick, *Jansenism*, pp. 23–27.

38. Van Kley, *Jansenists*, pp. 11–12.

39. Sedgwick, *Jansenism*, pp. 28–31.

40. Sedgwick, *Jansenism*, p. 44.

41. Weaver, *Evolution*, p. 63.

42. The five propositions are: (1) some of God's commandments are impossible for the just who wish and endeavor to obey them, considering the forces they possess; the grace that would make their fulfillment possible is also lacking; (2) in the state of fallen nature, no one ever resists interior grace; (3) to merit or demerit in the state of fallen nature, it is not necessary that we be free from internal necessity; it is sufficient that we be free from external constraint; (4) the semi-Pelagians admitted the necessity of an interior prevenient grace for every action, but they were heretical in that they held that this grace was such that we could either obey or resist it; and (5) to hold that Jesus Christ died or shed his blood for all humanity, without excepting anyone, is semi-Pelagianism. These propositions are available in many sources; see, for example, Charles-Augustin Sainte-Beuve, *Port-Royal* Volume 1 (Paris: Gallimand, 1951), pp. 580–584.

43. The text of the formulary reads as follows. "I submit sincerely to the constitution of Pope Innocent X of May 31, 1653, according to its true meaning, which was determined by the constitution of our Holy Father, Pope Alexander VII, on October 16, 1656. I recognize that I am obliged in

conscience to obey these constitutions, and I condemn in heart and speech the doctrine of the five propositions of Cornelius Jansenius, contained in his book entitled *Augustinus*, which these two popes and the bishops have condemned; said doctrine not being that of Saint Augustine which Jansenius has ill-interpreted, contrary to the true meaning of the Doctor." See Escholier, *Port-Royal*, p. 315.

44. Alexander Sedgwick, "Jansen and the Jansenists," *History Today* 40 (July 1990), p. 41.

45. Sedgwick, *Jansenism*, pp. x–xi.

46. F. Ellen Weaver, "Cloister and Salon in Seventeenth Century Paris: Introduction to a Study in Women's History," *Ohio Journal of Religious Studies* 4 (March 1976), p. 45.

47. F. Ellen Weaver, "Angélique de Saint-Jean of Port-Royal: The 'Third Superior' as 'Mythographer' in the Dynamics of Reform Caught in Controversy," in E. R. Elder, ed., *Cistercians in the Late Middle Ages* (Kalamazoo: Cistercian Publications, 1981), p. 91.

48. Jean LeClerq, "A Sociological Approach to the History of a Religious Order," in M. Basil Pennington, ed., *The Cistercian Spirit* (Kalamazoo, MI: Cistercian Publications, 1970), pp. 134–143.

49. F. Ellen Weaver, "Histories and Historians of Port-Royal," in J. E. Booty, ed., *The Divine Drama in History and Liturgy* (Allison Park, IL: Pickwick Publications, 1984), p. 46.

50. Weaver, "Angélique de Saint-Jean," pp. 94–95.

51. Weaver, "Angélique de Saint-Jean," p. 97. "Relation" is the term used to refer to the memoirs written by many of the nuns of Port-Royal during these troubling times.

52. Weaver notes that when the history of a community becomes the history of a *persecuted* community, then history becomes myth. She understands myth as "a metaphoric, a poetic, symbolic account of events of a heroic past which relates at a deep subconscious level to a psychological, *theological*, perception of reality shared by a cultural group. . . . At the core of the myth is historical fact. But this historical core is less important than the perception of reality beyond fact." Weaver, "Angélique de Saint-Jean," p. 98.

53. F. Ellen Weaver, "Erudition, Spirituality, and Women: The Jansenist Contribution," in S. Marshall, ed., *Women in Reformation and Counter-Reformation Europe* (Bloomington: Indiana University Press, 1989), p. 189.

54. Weaver, "Erudition," p. 191.

55. Weaver, "Erudition," p. 196.

56. Claude Lancelot, "*Relation du voyage d'Aleth*," National Archives of Utrecht, MS P. R. 8 (December 18, 1644), cited in Weaver, "Erudition," p. 196.

57. Dom Guéranger, *Institutions Liturgiques*, published in three volumes in Paris in 1860.

58. "*Appellants*" were those who had appealed to a general council in rejecting Pope Clement XI's 1713 bull, "*Unigenitus*," which condemned the five propositions in Quesnel's *Réflections morales*.

59. F. Ellen Weaver, "*Contribution des Port-Royalistes aux Liturgies Néo-Gallicanes*," *Chroniques de Port-Royal* No. 35 (1986), p. 178. (An English version of this article appeared later as "The Neo-Gallican Liturgies Revisited," *Studia Liturgica* 16 (1986/1987) Number 3/4, pp. 54–72.)

60. For a detailed discussion of the comparison between the Tridentine and Jansenist approaches to liturgical reform, see F. Ellen Weaver, "Jansenist Bishops and Liturgical-Social Reform," in J. M. Golden, ed., *Church, State, and Society under the Bourbon Kings of France* (Lawrence, KA: Coronado Press, Inc.), pp. 24–82.

61. For an overview of the connection between the Augustinianism of the Jansenists and their subsequent belief that both scripture and the liturgy were meant to be accessible to everyone, including the laity and even women, see F. Ellen Weaver, "Scripture and Liturgy for the Laity: The Jansenist Case for Translation," *Worship* 59 (1985), pp. 510–521.

62. See F. Ellen Weaver, "Liturgy for the Laity: The Jansenist Case for Popular Participation in Worship in the Seventeenth and Eighteenth Centuries," *The Jansenist* (January 1989), pp. 1–10.

63. Klauser, *Short History*, p. 121.

64. Weaver, "Neo-Gallican Liturgies," p. 67.

65. Sedgwick, *Jansenism*, p. x.

66. Escholier, *Port-Royal*, p. 307.

67. Weaver, *Evolution*, p. 93.

68. Weaver, *Evolution*, p. 94.

5

Connections: Honoring the Past, Envisioning the Future

This book began as a response to the women whose stories it tells. Scattered articles, the occasional video, and tantalizing chapters in more general texts led me to seek out more information about these women, in an attempt both to get to know them better and to understand the societies in which they lived. Always in the background, too, was F. Ellen Weaver's caveat that, perhaps, these women didn't "fit," didn't belong together. Finally, I started with a gut-level conviction that, once known, these women would have a lot to say to contemporary Christians about gospel living.

The quest has been rewarding on many levels. The period from the thirteenth to the eighteenth century was, in northwestern Europe as in other parts of the Christian world, a time of intense searching for new ways to be upon the earth. In religion as in society, old truths were confronting new realities and, like the wineskins in the parable, the basic fabrics of both institutions were bursting. The women we have met in these pages responded to all these things in ways at once unique and parallel, ways that spoke to them centuries ago and continue to speak to us today.

Yet the inevitable question again arises: "So what?" So what have we learned from four relatively obscure groups of relatively obscure women who lived in a period that many modern people consider perhaps colorful, perhaps even a bit interesting or romantic, but certainly not relevant in a post-scientific, largely cynical, profit-driven world? We have, in fact, learned quite a bit.

THE WOMEN

We have, first of all, met four groups of very engaging, very courageous women. And one of the most engaging things about them is that they would never have thought of themselves as courageous at all. They were simply women of their day, whatever that particular day happened to be, striving to find the best way possible to live lives that reflected their own convictions about God, about the gospels, and about society.

The beguines devised a lifestyle that combined religious and secular life in a new and unique way. In so doing, they embodied the true spirit of biblical theology that holds that all of life is, ultimately, religious because all of life is filled with the Creator. These "out-of-order" women challenged, however unconsciously, existing ecclesiastical and societal limitations, and created a new form of women's spirituality.

The Anabaptists absorbed the gospels so completely that their tremendous commitment, which we see as so awesome, was, for them, quite simple—live the gospel and accept the consequences. They did not set out to be martyrs but the threat of death could not shake them from their resolve. Perhaps more than the other women here, the women of the Anabaptist movement purposefully steeped themselves in the scriptures, finding in them both a guide for living and a purpose for dying.

The period of the witch craze is, perhaps, the most poignant in some ways since it involved so many women who probably didn't even understand what they had done to be treated so horribly. The nuns of Port-Royal serve as a warning against harsh judgments that are rooted in a lack of openness to various interpretations of scripture and church teaching.

HISTORICAL CONTEXT

It would be impossible to learn about, much less learn from, these women if we did not at the same time recognize the critical importance of studying movements against the backdrop of the historical periods in which they arose, during which they flourished, and, finally, against which they faded.

In the cases of the women in this book, common factors include sudden and tremendous population spurts and shifts, the emergence of the guild system, the rise of nationalism, the various movements of reform and revolt, the invention of the printing press, the nascient stirrings of the scientific revolution, and of course, the "women's question," the fact that, during much of this time, women in western Europe simply outnumbered men.

ECCLESIASTICAL DEVELOPMENTS

During the period being examined here, many of the ecclesiastical developments had to do with power: the growing centralization of authority in the person of the pope; the increasing influence of the curia surrounding the pope; the conviction that true unity could only be found in a rigid uniformity; and, perhaps most disastrously, the creation of the Inquisition with its terrible but effective system for rooting out and dealing with "heretics."

More positive developments in Christianity during this time were, for the most part, happening outside the official hierarchical structures, among the emerging mendicant orders, such as the Franciscans, and with individual reformers who, however unwittingly, paved the way for the great divisions of the sixteenth century. Our women all represent different stages and forms of this quest for spiritual renewal and revival that inevitably set them at odds with ecclesiastical authority. One of the great "What if's" of medieval Christianity is, "What if those who held official power in western Christianity at this time were more concerned with true reform and less concerned with plurality of practice?"

AN INTRIGUING QUESTION

Despite the differences among them, these four groups of women lived in generally the same geographical location and felt the same stirrings to search for deeper forms of spirituality or, in the case of the so-called witches, to maintain a simpler form of Christianity. They all, in one form or another, managed to rouse the suspicion of the official church. They all suffered for their beliefs, some quite horribly, and thousands died terrible deaths.

Why? This is not a rhetorical question, but it is one that this book has not been able to answer. Much more research remains to be done about the general atmosphere in this part of western Europe during this period. Many places were experiencing some form of lay spiritual awakening. Why was the official response in the northern tier so much more ferocious and unforgiving than it apparently was in other parts of Europe?

It would be instructive to map out the houses of the beguines, the sites of the Anabaptist martyrdoms, and the squares where the so-called witches were burned, to see if there is a high degree of correlation. I suspect there is. Nor would the Paris of the nuns of Port-Royal be unimportant here, since Marguerite Porete was also burned in Paris. Was it the harsher climate of the north that led to harsher judgments? Do rougher terrains breed rougher minds that see no other way to deal with perceived opposition than to stamp it out? These are evocative questions, but they remain beyond the scope of the present study.

AND WHAT OF US?

On December 2, 1980, four American churchwomen were raped and murdered in El Salvador. Maryknoll sisters Maura Clarke and Ita Ford, lay missioner Jean Donovan, and Ursuline sister Dorothy Kazel took the gospel seriously and paid the ultimate price for their commitment. Referring to Maura, Ita, and Carla Piette, who also had died in El Salvador that fateful year, Judith Noone observes: "The manner and moments of their deaths were extraordinary for most of us from the U.S. because we were not attuned to the reality of martyrdom in our world today."[1]

Why? Why should the deaths of a handful of Americans come as a surprise? Perhaps we were not "attuned to the reality of martyrdom" because we have chosen to believe that the freedom and abundance available to most Americans is somehow ours by right. Perhaps we have allowed ourselves to shut out the real sufferings endured by the majority of people in today's world, where most of the resources are reserved for, and consumed by, a tiny minority of the global population.

Perhaps, too, because most of us have no patience with history. Learning about the past is, we tell ourselves, tedious and boring and takes up precious time that could be more profitably spent in the pursuit of money, power, and pleasure. But our ignorance of the past leaves us less able both to understand and cope with the present and to envision and create a better future. Christians in particular need to steep themselves in the stories of those who came before and in the realities of the first two Christian millennia, to admire the good, to be honest about the bad, and to resolve anew to chart a clearer path in the coming decades.

One of the bits of dialogue in *Celebrate Life!*, a musical interpretation of the gospels, concerns the disciples' utter inability to comprehend the death of Jesus. In the midst of the conversation, one of them asks plaintively whether people simply find love so horrible to look upon that they have to kill it.[2] That question echoes down the ages from Calvary to the stakes of the Inquisition to the rifles of El Salvador and the intolerant attitudes of so many today.

We must own the past. Even more importantly, we must enrich our understanding of the past by getting beyond the silences and re-discovering the women who played vital but unheralded roles in the development of western Christianity.

Listening for the remains of "lesser lives" in the ancient world requires an ef-fort to undo many centuries of silence, misinterpretation and ignorance.[3] Attempting to hear the voices or even the echoes of women in the origins of Christianity means listening for resonances of those who were unheard in the past, and who have been further silenced not only by design but also by neglect.[4]

We must challenge the assumptions of the patriarchal system that has been in control of western civilization for so many centu-ries. Even women trained in theology were, at first, trained by exclu-sively male mentors. In my own case, it took me several years to realize that nothing in my formal course work had prepared me to open up the women's stories, the "underside" of Christian history. Like many women theologians, I was the product of male training, nor am I lamenting that. Most of my mentors were good, coura-geous, intellectually honest men. Still, it was left to me to find my own way. Were it not for an article in the Sunday magazine section of the *Philadelphia Inquirer* newspaper, I might never have stumbled on the beguines, been fascinated by them, and begun my personal quest for the unheralded women I now hold so dear. So we must con-sciously and conscientiously set aside what Mary Rose D'Angelo calls our patriarchal reflexes, those "reflexes acquired by living with patriarchy [which] are perfectly adequate to accomplish their goals without needing attention from the conscious mind."[5]

It is, then, only by a conscious listening, a conscious reading, a conscious searching that we will be able to overcome the silences and the historical gaps. The women presented here, no longer com-pletely unheralded, point the direction. It is up to us to follow their lead.

NOTES

1. Judith M. Noone, *The Same Fate as the Poor* (Maryknoll: Orbis Books, 1995, rev.), p. xiii.

2. *Celebrate Life!*, Ragan Courtney, lyrics, and Buryl Red, music (Nashville: Broadman, 1972).

3. Sandra R. Joshel, "Listening to Silence," in *Work, Identity and Legal Status at Rome: A Study of the Occupational Inscriptions* (Norman:University of Oklahoma Press, 1992), pp. 3–24.

4. Mary Rose D'Angelo, "Hardness of Hearing, Muted Voices: Listening for the Silences in History," in Mary Ann Hinsdale and Phyllis H. Kaminski, eds., *Women and Theology* (Maryknoll: Orbis Books, 1995), p. 83.

5. D'Angelo, "Hardness of Hearing," p. 85.

Glossary

Beguinages—the term given to the houses or complexes where laywomen called beguines lived a semi-communal life.

Benedictine Order—the confederation of monasteries adhering to the Rule of Benedict. Composed by Benedict of Nursia in the sixth century, the rule eventually spread throughout the Christian world.

Cistercians—monks in the Benedictine monastic tradition. Their name is derived from their foundation at Cîteaux, near Dijon, in the Burgundy region of France. The monks desired to follow the Rule of Benedict to the letter.

Council—an official gathering of Church leaders and representatives that assists with the process of decision making within the church. Ecumenical councils are supreme exercises of the collegial authority of bishops.

Council of Trent (1545–1563)—an ecumenical council called in response to the Protestant Reformation. By its conclusion the council had defined Catholic doctrine in a way that made the split with the Protestants irrevocable. "Tridentine" Catholicism endured until the second half of the twentieth century, finally yielding to the modern reforms of the Second Vatican Council (1963–1965).

Courtly Love—the medieval code of attitudes toward love and of the highly conventionalized conduct considered suitable for noble lords and ladies.

Crusades—a series of wars fought in the eleventh through thirteenth centuries under the banner of Christ for the recovery of or in defense of Christian lands.

Double Monasteries—monastic foundations, popular from the fourth to the twelfth century, comprised of both men and women. While strictly segregated in their living quarters, men and women shared common liturgical facilities and were normally under the rule of a woman superior. Their eventual suppression has been attributed to ecclesiastical uneasiness with powerful women superiors.

Gallicanism—an eccesiology that claimed for France the right to resist all but very restricted forms of papal intervention within its jurisdiction.

Gregorian Reform—a movement of renewal in the Western church beginning in the tenth century but associated with its most ardent champion, Pope Gregory VII (1073–1085).

Heresy—the post-baptismal denial of the truth of a dogma, that is, a teaching that has been proposed as divinely revealed.

Humanism—a modern philosophical worldview marked by cultural pluralism, an optimistic view of human nature, and an emphasis on the post-Enlightenment virtues of rationality, equality, and freedom.

Inquisition—an institution in Catholicism for the eradication and punishment of heresy. Established in 1542, the institution was renamed in 1965 by Pope Paul VI as the Congregation for the Doctrine of the Faith, a branch of the Roman Curia.

Jansenism—a seventeenth-century Catholic reform movement originating in the Low Countries and France. Jansenism was pessimistic about human nature without God's grace, demanded strict asceticism, fought the centralizing tendencies of Tridentine Catholicism, and opposed French absolutism.

Justinian Code—a revision of Roman law published by the emperor Justinian I (483–565) in 529. The code was influential in the later development and understanding of canon (church) law.

Malleus Maleficarum (Hammer against the Witches)—a handbook written in 1486 to guide those involved in the apprehension and conviction of witches.

Monasticism—an institutionalized form of ascetic religious life in which individuals take vows of poverty, chastity, and obedience, and, in some orders, stability. The goal of monasticism is to pursue, through a formal rule, a life of prayer and work for the glory of God and the good of the church and the world.

Papal Bull—a papal document that affects matters of import for a substantial portion of the church. The term "bull" comes from the Latin *bulla*, the lead seal that authenticates the document.

Peasants' War (1524–1525)—a rebellion in Germany against the Catholic Church and feudal lords.

Roman Curia—the bureaucracy that assists the pope in the responsibilities of governing the universal church. The Curia is organized into offices of various ranks and importance; chief among them is the Secretariat of State.

Schism—a formal breach of church unity brought about when a particular group willfully separates itself from the larger faith community.

Scholasticism—a method of intellectual inquiry that was prominent until the sixteenth century in Western medieval thought, especially in the universities. Unlike the monastic approach, which reflected meditatively on the Bible, scholasticism wrestled with the texts themselves, using the technique of questions and answers.

Solitaires—a group of men who attached themselves to the Monastery of Port-Royal in Paris in the seventeenth century.

Summa Theologica—the Synthesis of Theology, Thomas Aquinas' most important systematic work in theology, written in the thirteenth century.

Bibliography

GENERAL

Anderson, Bonnie S. and Judith P. Zinsse. *A History of Their Own: Europe from Prehistory to the Present.* Volume 1. New York: Harper & Row, 1988.

Armstrong, Karen. *The Gospel According to Woman: Christianity's Creation of the Sex War in the West.* New York: Doubleday, 1987.

Bellamy, J. *Crime and Public Order in England in the Later Middle Ages.* London: Routledge and Kegan Paul, 1973.

Boulding, Elise. *The Underside of History: A View of Women through Times.* Boulder, CO: Westview Press, 1976.

Bynum, Caroline Walker. *Holy Feast and Holy Fast: The Religious Significance of Food to Medieval Women.* Berkeley: University of California Press, 1987.

Celebrate Life! Ragan Courtney, lyrics. Buryl Red, music. Nashville: Broadman, 1972.

Clark, Elizabeth, and Herbert Richardon. *Women and Religion: A Feminist Sourcebook of Christian Thought.* San Francisco: Harper San Francisco, 1977.

D'Angelo, Mary Rose. "Hardness of Hearing, Muted Voices: Listening for the Silences in History." In Mary Ann Hinsdale and Phyllis H. Kaminski, eds. *Women and Theology.* Maryknoll: Orbis Books, 1995.

Desmons, Giles, *Walking Paris: Thirty Original Walks in and Around Paris.* Lincolnwood, IL: Passport Books, 1997.

Ennen, Edith. *The Medieval Woman.* Edmund Jephcott, trans. Oxford: Basil Blackwell Ltd., 1989.

Ferguson, Everett, ed. *Encyclopedia of Early Christianity.* New York: Garland Publishing, Inc., 1990.

Herlihy, David. *The Social Hstory of Italy and Western Europe 700–1500: Collected Studies.* London: Various Reprints, 1979.

Joshel, Sandra R. "Listening to Silence." In *Work, Identity and Legal Status at Rome: A Study of the Occupational Inscriptions.* Norman: University of Oklahoma Press, 1992.

King, Margaret L. *Women of the Renaissance.* Chicago: The University of Chicago Press, 1991.

Klauser, Theodore. *A Short History of the Western Liturgy.* Second Edition. Oxford: Oxford University Press, 1978.

Little, Lester L. *Religious Poverty and the Profit Economy in Medieval Europe.* Ithaca, NY: Cornell University Press, 1978.

McBrien, Richard P. *Catholicism: Study Edition.* New York: Harper & Row, 1981.

———. *The Harpercollins Encyclopedia of Catholicism.* San Francisco Harper San Francisco, 1995.

Morris, Joan. *The Lady Was a Bishop: The Hidden History of Women with Clerical Ordination and the Jurisdiction of Bishops.* New York: The Macmillan Company, 1973.

Newman, Barbara. *From Virile Woman to Woman-Christ: Studies in Medieval Religion and Literature.* Philadelphia: The University of Pennsylvania Press, 1995.

Noone, Judith M. *The Same Fate as the Poor.* Maryknoll: Orbis Books, 1995, rev.

Oden, Amy. *In Her Words: Women's Writings in the History of Christian Thought.* Nashville: Abingdon Press, 1994.

Radford Ruether, Rosemary. *Women and Redemption: A Theological History.* Minneapolis: Fortress Press, 1998.

Rosenthal, Joel T. *Medieval Women and the Sources of Medieval History.* Athens: The University of Georgia Press, 1990.

Southern, R. W. *Western Society and the Church in the Middle Ages.* The Pelican History of the Church. Volume Two. Baltimore: Penguin Books, 1973.

Strayer, Joseph R., ed. *Dictionary of the Middle Ages.* New York: Charles Scribner's Sons, 1983.

BEGUINES

Bloch, Mark. *La Société féodale.* Paris: Ablin Michel, 1994.

Bogert, C. "What If There Were None?" *Newsweek.* Dec. 26, 1994/Jan. 2, 1995.

Bolton, Brenda M. *"Mulieres Sanctae."* In Derek Brown, ed. *Sanctity and Secularity: The Church and the World.* Studies in Church History. Volume 10. New York: Barnes & Noble Books, 1973, pp. 77–95.

Bryant, Gwendolyn. "The French Heretic Marguerite Porete." In Katharina M. Wilson, ed. *Medieval Women Writers*. Athens: University of Georgia Press, 1984, pp. 200–215.

Bynum, Caroline Walker. "Women Mystics and Eucharistic Devotion in the Thirteenth Century." *Women's Studies* 11 (1984): 179–214.

Chenu, Marie-Dominique. *Nature, Man, and Society in the Twelfth Century*. Jerome Taylor and Lester K. Little, ed./trans. Chicago: The University of Chicago Press, 1968.

DeGanck, Roger. *Beatrice of Nazareth in Her Context*. Kalamazoo, MI: Cistercian Publications, 1991.

Devlin, Dennis. "Feminine Lay Piety in the High Middle Ages: The Beguines." In J. A. Nichols and L. T. Shank, eds. *Distant Echoes: Medieval Religious Women*. Volume One. Kalamazoo, MI: Cistercian Publications, 1984, pp. 183–196.

Erickson, Carolly. *The Medieval Vision: Essays in History and Perception*. New York: Oxford University Press, 1976.

Furlong, Monica. *Visions & Longings: Medieval Women Mystics*. Boston: Shambhala Publications, Inc., 1996.

Grundmann, Herbert. *Religiöse Bewegungen in Mittelalter: Untersuchungen über die geschichtlichen Zusammenhange zwischen der ketzerei, 12. und 13. In Jahrhundert und die geschichtlichen Grundiagen der deutschen Mystik*. Berlin, 1935.

Hoornaert, R. *The Beguinage of Bruges: The Vineyard Then and Now*. P. A. Bennett, trans. Ostend: 1988.

Idel, Moseh, and Bernard McGinn. *Mysticism and Monotheistic Faith: An Ecumenical Dialogue*. New York: Macmillan Publishing Co., 1989.

Koorn, Florence. "Women Without Vows: The Case of the Beguines and the Sisters of the Common Life in the Northern Netherlands." In Anne MacLachlan, trans. and Elisja Schulte van Kessel, ed. *Women and Men in Spiritual Culture: XIV–XVII Centuries*. The Hague: Netherlands Government Publishing Office, 1984, pp. 135–147.

Lerner, Robert E. "Beguines and Beghards." In Joseph Strayer, ed. *Dictionary of the Middle Ages*. Volume 2. New York: Scribner, 1992, pp. 157–162.

———. *The Heresy of the Free Spirit in the Late Middle Ages*. Los Angeles: University of California Press, 1972.

McDonnell, Ernest W. *The Beguines and Beghards in Medieval Culture with Special Emphasis on the Belgian Scene*. New Brunswick, NJ: Rutgers University Press, 1954.

McNamara, Jo Ann Kay. *Sisters in Arms: Catholic Nuns through Two Millennia*. Cambridge, MA: Harvard University Press, 1996.

———. "*De Quibusdam Mulieribus*: Reading Women's History from Hostile Sources." In Joel T. Rosenthal, ed. *Medieval Women and the Sources of Medieval History*. Athens: The University of Georgia Press, 1990.

"Memorandum Presented to the Delegates of the Bishop of Tournai in Favor of the Beguinage of Saint Elisabeth in Ghent." In J. Béthune, ed. *Cartulaire du béguinage de Sainte Elisabeth à Ghent.* Bruges: Aimé de Zuttere, 1883.

Neel, Carol. "The Origin of the Beguines." In Judith M. Bennett, Elizabeth A. Clark, Jean F. O'Barr, Anne Vilen, and Sarah Westphal-Wihl, eds. *Sisters and Workers in the Middle Ages.* Chicago: The University of Chicago Press, 1989, pp. 241–260.

Peters, Marygrace. "Beguine Women: Medieval Spirituality, Modern Implications." *Review for Religious,* March–April 1995, pp. 244–236.

Petroff, Elizabeth Alvilda. *Body and Soul Essays on Medieval Women and Mysticism.* New York: Oxford University Press, 1994.

Philippen, L.J.M. *De Begijhoven, Oorsprong, Geschiedenis, Inrichting.* Antwerp: Veritas, 1918.

Pierre Maes, Pierre. *"Les Béguinages."* In *Trésors des Beguinages.* Ghent: Musée des Beaux Arts, 1961.

Porete, Marguerite. *The Mirror of Simple Souls.* Ellen L. Babinsky, trans. New York: Crossroad, 1993.

Power, E. "The Position of Women." In C. G. Crump and E. F. Jacob, eds. *The Legacy of the Middle Ages.* Oxford: Oxford University Press, 1962.

Prose, Francine. "Ancient Beguinages of Flanders." *The New York Times Magazine,* October 21, 1990, pp. 26–27, 44, 46–47.

Simons, Walter. "The Beguine Movement in the Southern Low Countries: A Reassessment." *Bulletin de l'Institut Historique Belge de Rome/Bulletin van het Belgisch Historisch Institut te Rome* 59 (1989): 63–105.

Verdeyen, Paul. *"Le Procès d'inquisition contre Marguerite Porete et Guiard de Cressonessart (1309–1310)."* *Revue d'histoire ecclésiastique* 81 (1986): 47–94.

Wilson, Katharina M., ed. *Medieval Women Writers.* Athens: University of Georgia Press, 1984.

Ziegler, Joanna E. *Sculpture of Compassion: The Pietà and the Beguines in the Southern Low Countries c. 1300–c. 1600.* Brussels: Institut historique belge de Rome, 1992.

———. "Women of the Middle Ages: Some Questions Regarding the Beguines and Devotional Art." *Vox Benedictina* 3, 4 (October 1986): 338–357.

Zum Brunn, Emilie, and Georgette Epiney Burgard. *Women Mystics in Medieval Europe.* New York: Paragon House, 1989.

ANABAPTISTS

Bainton, Roland H. *The Reformation of the Sixteenth Century.* Boston: Beacon Press, 1952.

———. *Women of the Reformation in Germany and Italy.* Minneapolis: Augsburg Publishing House, 1971.

Barrett, Lois. "The Role and Influence of Anabaptist Women in the Martyr Story." *Brethren Life and Thought* 37 (Spring 1992): 87–96.

Bax, E. Belfort. *Rise and Fall of the Anabaptists.* Reprint. New York: Augustus M. Kelley Publishers, 1970 [1903].

Bender, Harold S. "The Anabaptists and Religious Liberty in the 16th Century." *Archiv für Reformationsgeschichte* 44 (1953): 32–51.

Clasen, Claus-Peter. *Anabaptism: A Social History, 1525–1618.* Ithaca, NY: Cornell University Press, 1972.

Dyck, Cornelius J., ed. *An Introduction to Mennonite History: A Popular History of the Anabaptists and the Mennonites.* Scottdale, PA: Herald Press, 1981.

———. "The Suffering Church in Anabaptism." *Mennonite Quarterly Review* 59, 1 (January 1985): 5–23.

Estep, William R. *The Anabaptist Story: An Introduction to Sixteenth-Century Anabaptism.* 3rd Edition. Grand Rapids, MI: William B. Eerdmans Publishing Company, 1996.

Ferguson, Everett, ed. *Encyclopedia of Early Christianity.* New York: Garland Publishing, Inc., 1990.

Friedmann, Robert. "Leonhard Schiemer and Hans Schlaffer: Two Tyrolean Anabaptist Martyr-Apostles," *Mennonite Quarterly Review* 33 (1959): 31–41.

———. *The Theology of Anabaptists.* Scottdale, PA: Herald Press, 1973.

George, Timothy. "Early Anabaptist Spirituality in the Low Countries." *Mennonite Quarterly Review* 62, 3 (July 1988): 257–275.

Goertz, Hans-Jürgen. *The Anabaptists.* Second Edition. New York: Routledge, 1988.

Gross, Leonard. "Recasting the Anabaptist Vision: The Longer View." *Mennonite Quarterly Review* 60 (July 1986): 352–363.

Keeney, W. E. *Dutch Anabaptist Thought and Practice 1539–1564.* Nieuwkoop: B. de Graaf, 1968.

Klassen, Herbert C. "Ambrosius Spittelmayr: His Life and Teachings." *Mennonite Quarterly Review* 32 (1958): 251–271.

Klassen, John. "Women and the Family among Dutch Anabaptist Martyrs." *Mennonite Quarterly Review* 60 (1986): 548–571.

Klassen, Walter, ed. *Anabaptism Revisited.* Scottdale, PA: Herald Press, 1992.

Kreider, Alan. "The Relevance of *Martyrs' Mirror* to Our Time." *Mennonite Life* (September 1990): 21–28.

Liechty, Daniel, trans./ed. *Early Anabaptist Spirituality: Selected Writings.* New York: Paulist Press, 1994.

Lindberg, Carter. *The European Reformations.* Cambridge, MA: Blackwell Publishers, Inc., 1996.

Littell, Franklin H. *The Anabaptist View of the Church.* Second Edition. Boston: Beacon Hill, 1958.

Nyce, Dorothy Yoder. "Are Anabaptists Motherless?" In Dorothy Nyce, ed. *Which Way Women?* Akron, PA: Mennonite Central Committee Peace Section, 1980, pp. 122–129.

Packull, Werner O. "Anna Jansz of Rotterdam, a Historical Investigation of an Early Anabaptist Martyr." *Archiv für Reformationsgeschichte* 78 (1987): 147–173.

Payne, Ernest A. "The Anabaptists." In G. R. Elton, ed. *The New Cambridge Modern History.* Volume II: The Reformation 1520–1559. Cambridge: Cambridge University Press, 1962.

Plenert, Wayne. "The Martyr's Mirror and Anabaptist Women." *Mennonite Life* (June 1975): 13–18.

Sprunger, Keith L. "God's Powerful Army of the Weak: Anabaptist Women of the Radical Reformation." In R. L. Greaves, ed. *Triumph over Silence: Women in Protestant History.* Westport, CT: Greenwood Press, 1985, pp. 45–74.

Stauffer, Ethelbert. "The Anabaptist Theology of Martyrdom." *Mennonite Quarterly Review* 19 (1945): 179–214.

Studer, Gerald C. "A History of the *Martyrs' Mirror.*" *Mennonite Quarterly Review* 22 (1948): 163–179.

Swartzentruber, A. Orly. "The Piety and Theology of the Anabaptist Martyrs in van Braght's *Martyrs' Mirror.*" *Mennonite Quarterly Review* 28 (1954): 129–142.

Umble, Jenifer Hiett. "Women and Choice: An Examination of the *Martyrs' Mirror.*" *Mennonite Quarterly Review* 64 (April 1990): 135–145.

van Braght, Tielman J. *The Bloody Theatre or Martyrs' Mirror of the Defenseless Christians.* Translated from the edition of 1660 by J. F. Sohm. Scottdale, PA: Herald Press, 1950.

von Beck, Josef, ed. *Die Geschichts-Bücher der Wiedertäufer in Oesterreich-Ungarn.* Vienna: Carl Gerold's Sohn, 1883.

Wedel, Coendrius H. *Abruss der Geschicte der Mennoniten.* Newton, KS: Schulverlag von Bethel-College, 1900–1904.

Wenger, John C. *Even Unto Death: The Heroic Witness of the Sixteenth-Century Anabaptists.* Richmond, VA: John Knox Press, 1961.

White, James F. *Protestant Worship: Traditions in Transition.* Louisville, KY: Westminster-John Knox Press, 1989.

Williams, George Huntston. *The Radical Reformation.* Philadelphia: The Westminster Press, 1962.

Wyntjes, Sherrin Marshall. "Women and Religious Choices in the Sixteenth Century Netherlands." *Archiv für Reformationsgeschichte* 75 (1984): 276–289.

Yoder, John H. *The Legacy of Michael Sattler.* Scottdale, PA: Herald Press, 1973.

WITCH-HUNTS

Achterberg, Jeanne. *Woman as Healer.* Boston: Shambhala, 1991.

Adler, Margot. *Drawing Down the Moon.* New York: Beacon Press, 1979.

Anglo, Sydney. "Evident Authority and Authoritative Evidence: The *Malleus Maleficarum.*" In Sydney Anglo, ed. *The Damned Art: Essays in the Literature of Witchcraft.* London: Routledge & Kegan Paul, 1977, pp. 1–31.

Ankarloo, Bengt, and Gustav Henningsen, eds. *Early Modern European Witchcraft: Centres and Peripheries.* Oxford: Clarendon Press, 1993.

Baroja, Julio Caro. "Witchcraft and Catholic Theology." In Bengt Ankarloo and Gustav Henningsen, eds. *Early Modern European Witchcraft: Centres and Peripheries.* Oxford: Clarendon Press, 1993.

Barstow, Anne Llewellyn. "On Studying Witchcraft as Women's History." *Journal of Feminist Studies in Religion* 4 (Fall 1988): 7–19.

———. *Witchcraze: A New History of the European Witch Hunts.* San Francisco: Pandora, 1994.

Briggs, Robin. *Witches & Neighbors: The Social and Cultural Context of European Witchcraft.* New York: Penguin Books, 1996.

Burman, Edward. *The Inquisition: The Hammer of Heresy.* New York: Dorset Press, 1984.

"The Burning Times." Video. Part Two of the series, *Women and Spirituality.* The National Film Board of Canada, 1990.

Clark, Stuart. "Inversion, Misrule and the Meaning of Witchcraft." *Past and Present* 87 (May 1980): 98–127.

Dickson, M. G. "Patterns of European Sanctity: The Cult of Saints in the Later Middle Ages." Unpublished doctoral dissertation. University of Edinburgh, 1974.

Easlea, Brian. *Witch-Hunting Magic & the New Philosophy: An Introduction to Debates of the Scientific Revolution 1450–1750.* Atlantic Highlands, NJ: Humanities Press, Inc., 1980.

Ellerbe, Helen. *The Dark Side of Christian History.* San Rafael, CA: Morningstar Books, 1995.

Engel, Mary Potter. "Historical Theology and Violence against Women: Unearthing a Popular Tradition of Just Battery." In Mary Potter Engel and Walter E. Wyman, eds. *Revisioning the Past: Prospects in Historical Theology.* Minneapolis: Fortress Press, 1992, pp. 51–76.

Estes, Leland L. "Reginald Scott and his *Discoverie of Witchcraft*: Religion and Science in the Opposition to the European Witch Craze." *Church History* 52:6 (December 1983): 444–456.

Geis, Gilbert, and Ivan Bunn. *A Trial of Witches: A Seventeenth-Century Witchcraft Prosecution.* London: Routledge, 1997.

Gijswijt, Hofstra. "The European Witchcraft Debate and the Dutch Variant." *Social History* 15 (May 1990): 181–194.

Ginzburg, Carlo. *The Night Battles: Witchcraft and Agrarian Cults in the Sixteenth and Seventeenth Centuries.* John and Anne Tedeschi, trans. Baltimore: The Johns Hopkins University Press, 1992.

Hester, Marianne. *Lewd Women & Wicked Witches: A Study of the Dynamics of Male Domination.* London: Routledge, 1992.

Horsley, Richard A. "Who Were the Witches? The Social Roles of the Accused in the European Witch Trials." *Journal of Interdisciplinary History* 9:4 (Spring 1979): 23–42.

Jantzen, Grace M. *Power, Gender and Christian Mysticism.* New York: Cambridge University Press, 1995.

Kieckhefer, Richard. "The Holy and the Unholy: Sainthood, Witchcraft, and Magic in Late Medieval Europe." *Journal of Medieval and Renaissance Studies* 24 (Fall 1994): 355–385.

Kraemer, Heinrich, and Jakob Sprenger. *Malleus Maleficarum.* Montague Summers, trans. London: Pushkin Press, 1948.

Larner, Christina. *Witchcraft and Religion: The Politics of Popular Belief.* Oxford: Basil Blackwell Publisher Ltd., 1984.

Middelfort, H. C. Erik. "Witch Hunting and the Domino Theory." In James Obelkevich, ed. *Religion and the People, 800–1700.* Chapel Hill: University of North Carolina Press, 1979, pp. 277–288.

Monter, E. William. "The Pedestal and the Stake: Courtly Love and Witchcraft." In Renate Bridenthal and Claudia Koonz, eds. *Becoming Visible: Women in European History.* Boston: Houghton Mifflin Company, 1977, pp. 119–136.

Muchembled, Robert. "The Witches of the Cambrésis: The Acculturation of the Rural World in the Sixteenth and Seventeenth Centuries." In James Obelkevich, ed. *Religion and the People, 800–1700.* Chapel Hill: University of North Carolina Press, 1979, pp. 221–276.

Radford Ruether, Rosemary. "The Persecution of Witches: A Case of Sexism and Agism?" *Christianity and Crisis* December 23, 1974, pp. 291–295.

Richardson, Herbert W. *Nun, Witch, Playmate: The Americanization of Sex.* New York: Harper & Row, 1971.

Robbins, Russell Hope. *The Encyclopedia of Witchcraft and Demonology.* New York: Bonanza Books, 1981.

Russell, Jeffrey Burton. *Witchcraft in the Middle Ages.* Ithaca, NY: Cornell University Press, 1971.

Shannon, Albert C. *The Medieval Inquisition.* Second Edition. Collegeville, MI: The Liturgical Press, 1991.

Tedeschi, John. "Inquisitorial Law and the Witch." In Bengt Ankarloo and Gustave Henningsen, eds. *Early Modern European Witchcraft: Centres and Peripheries.* Oxford: Clarendon Press, 1993.

Trevor-Roper, Hugh R. *The European Witch-Craze of the Sixteenth and Seventeenth Centuries and Other Essays.* New York: Harper Torchbooks, 1967.

———. "Witches and Witchcraft: An Historical Essay." *Encounter* 28 (1967): 3–25.

———. "Witches and Witchcraft: An Historical Essay (II)." *Encounter* 28 (1967): 13–34.

Walker, Barbara. *The Woman's Encyclopedia of Myths and Secrets.* San Francisco: Harper & Row, 1983.

Williams, Marty, and Anne Echols. *Between Pit and Pedestal: Women in the Middle Ages.* Princeton: Markus Wiener Publishers, 1994.

"Witches." Video. A&E Series, *Ancient Mysteries,* 1996.

PORT-ROYAL

Ambercrombie, Nigel. "Mère Angélique and Port-Royal." *The Downside Review* 68 (July 1950): 341–352.

Chédozeau, Pierre. *"Port-Royal, les Gallicans et les Politiques à la Veille de la Déclaration des quatre Articles (1679–1681)."* *Revue des Sciences Philosophiques et Théologiques* 77 (1993): 533–546.

Cognet, Louis. *Post-Reformation Spirituality.* New York: Hawthorn Books, 1959.

Cwiekowski, Frederick J. "Gallicanism." In Joseph A. Komonchak et al., eds. *The New Dictionary of Theology*. Wilmington, DE: Michael Glazier, Inc., 1987.

Desmons, Giles. *Walking Paris: Thirty Original Walks in and Around Paris*. Lincolnwood, IL: Passport Books, 1997.

Dorival, Bernard. *"Le Jansénism et l'Art Français."* Bulletin de la Société des Amis de Port-Royal (1952): 3–13.

Dubois, E. T. "A Jesuit History of Jansenism." *Modern Language Review* 64:4 (1964): 764–773.

Émile, Jacques. *"Antoine Arnaud Défenseur de Jansénius."* In Edmond J. M. van Ejil, ed. *L'image de C. Jansénius jusqu'à la fin du 18e siècle: Actes du Colloque Louvain, november 1985*. Leuven: Leuven University Press, 1987, pp. 66–76.

Escholier, Marc. *Port-Royal: The Drama of the Jansenists*. New York: Hawthorn Books, Inc., 1968.

Franklin, R. W. "Guéranger and Variety in Unity." *Worship* 51:5 (September 1977): 378–399.

Hazelton, Roger. "Pascal and the Theology of Port-Royal." *Religion in Life* 3 (Summer 1958): 427–437.

Lachenmann, Eugen. "Port-Royal." In Samuel M. Jackson, ed. *The New Schaff-Herzog Encyclopedia of Religious Knowledge*. New York: McGraw Hill Book Company, 1967.

Lancelot, Claude. *"Relation du voyale d'Aleth."* National Archives of Utrecht. MS P. R. 8, December 18, 1644.

LeClerq, Jean. "A Sociological Approach to the History of a Religious Order." In M. Basil Pennington, ed. *The Cistercian Spirit*. Kalamazoo, MI: Cistercian Publications, 1970, pp. 134–143.

Lesaulnier, J. *"Jansénius et Plusieurs Amis de Port-Royal."* In Edmond J. M. van Ejil, ed. *L'image de C. Jansénius jusqu'à la fin du 18e siècle: Actes du Colloque Louvain, november 1985*. Leuven: Leuven University Press, 1987, pp. 77–92.

Nadler, Steven. "Cartesianism and Port-Royal." *Monist* 71 (October 1988): 573–584.

Sainte-Beuve, Charles-Augustin. *Port-Royal*. Volume 1. Paris: Gallimand, 1951.

Sedgwick, Alexander. "Jansen and the Jansenists." *History Today* 40 (July 1990): 36–42.

———. *Jansenism in Seventeenth-Century France: Voices from the Wilderness*. Charlottesville: University Press of Virginia, 1977.

———. "The Nuns of Port-Royal: A Study of Female Spirituality in Seventeenth-Century France." In Lynda L. Coon, Katherine J. Haldane, and Elisabeth W. Sommer, eds. *That Gentle Strength: Historical Perspectives on Women in Christianity*. Charlottesville: University Press of Virginia, 1990, pp. 1–25.

St. Cyres. "Jansenism." In James Hastings, ed. *Encyclopedia of Religion and Ethics*. New York: Charles Scribner's Sons.

Van Kley, Dale. *The Jansenists and the Expulsion of the Jesuits from France 1757–1765*. New Haven: Yale University Press, 1975.

Weaver, F. Ellen, "Angélique de Saint-Jean of Port-Royal: The 'Third Superior' as 'Mythographer' in the Dynamics of Reform Caught in Controversy." In E. R. Edler, ed. *Cistercians in the Late Middle Ages.* Kalamazoo, MI: Cistercian Publications, 1981, pp. 90–101.

———. "Cloister and Salon in Seventeenth Century Paris: Introduction to a Study in Women's History." *Ohio Journal of Religious Studies* 4 (March 1976): 44–57.

———. "*Contribution des Port-Royalistes aux Liturgies Néo-Gallicanes.*" *Chroniques de Port-Royal* 35 (1986): 171–194.

———. "Erudition, Spirituality, and Women: The Jansenist Contribution." In S. Marshall, ed. *Women in Reformation and Counter-Reformation Europe.* Bloomington: Indiana University Press, 1989, pp. 189–206.

———. *The Evolution of the Reform of Port-Royal: From the Rule of Cîteaux to Jansenism.* Paris: Éditions Beauchesne, 1978.

———. "Histories and Historians of Port-Royal." In J. E. Booty, ed. *The Divine Drama in History and Liturgy.* Allison Park, IL: Pickwick Publications, 1984, pp. 45–61.

———. "Jansenist Bishops and Liturgical-Social Reform." In J. M. Golden, ed. *Church, State, and Society under the Bourbon Kings of France.* Lawrence, KA: Coronado Press, Inc., pp. 24–82.

———. "Liturgy for the Laity: The Jansenist Case for Popular Participation in Worship in the Seventeenth and Eighteenth Centuries." *The Jansenist,* January 1989, pp. 1–10.

———. "Scripture and Liturgy for the Laity: The Jansenist Case for Translation." *Worship* 59 (1985): 510–521.

Index

About the Author

MARIE A. CONN is Associate Professor of Religious Studies at Chestnut Hill College in Philadelphia.